D0654540

Regency England

IN THE SAME SERIES

General Editors: Eric J. Evans and P.D. King

LANCASTER PAMPHLETS

Regency England

The age of Lord Liverpool

John Plowright

London and New York

First published 1996
by Routledge
2 Park Square, Milton Park, Abingdon, Oxon, OX14 4RN

Transferred to Digital Printing 2005

Simultaneously published in the USA and Canada
by Routledge
270 Madison Ave, New York NY 10016

© 1996 John Plowright

The moral right of the author has been asserted

Typeset in Bembo by
Ponting–Green Publishing Services, Chesham, Bucks

All rights reserved. No part of this book may be reprinted
or reproduced or utilized in any form or by any electronic,
mechanical, or other means, now known or hereafter
invented, including photocopying and recording, or in any
information storage or retrieval system, without
permission in writing from the publishers.

British Library Cataloguing in Publication Data

A catalogue record for this book is available from
the British Library

Library of Congress Cataloguing in Publication Data

A catalogue record for this book has been requested

ISBN 0–415–12140–X

To MY PARENTS

Contents

Foreword

Lancaster Pamphlets offer concise and up-to-date accounts of major historical topics, primarily for the help of students preparing for Advanced Level examinations, though they should also be of value to those pursuing introductory courses in universities and other institutions of higher education. Without being all-embracing, their aims are to bring some of the central themes or problems confronting students and teachers into sharper focus than the textbook writer can hope to do; to provide the reader with some of the results of recent research which the textbook may not embody; and to stimulate thought about the whole interpretation of the topic under discussion.

Acknowledgements

For their expert advice at every stage of this project I wish to express my thanks to Professor Eric J. Evans, Dr P.D. King and all the others concerned with the production of the *Lancaster Pamphlets* series. I would also like to thank Professor Jeremy Black, Mr David Gallop, Dr Jonathan Parry and Mr and Mrs G. W. Toulmin for their various forms of inspiration, encouragement and assistance. The Governing Body, Head Master, colleagues and students of Repton School also deserve thanks for providing conditions conducive to work. In so far as what follows may be deemed to possess any merit this is ultimately attributable to the teaching I received at the hands of Mr Ken Reed, Mr Maurice Cowling, Professor David Cannadine and Professor Derek Beales and is more immediately attributable to comments on earlier drafts of this piece by Professor Evans, Dr King, Miss Heather McCallum and Dr Parry. All the imperfections in what follows are, however, my own. Last, but not least, thanks are due to Sue, Alex and James for their forbearance when I wanted to work and for providing welcome distractions when I did not.

JP
Repton
June 1995

CHRONOLOGY

1811 Prince of Wales becomes Regent
Luddite disturbances begin
1812 The Framebreaking Act makes destruction of frames a capital offence
The Watch and Ward Act empowers the Nottingham authorities to appoint constables until 1 March 1814, if disturbances occurred or were feared
Luddite disturbances peak with the attack on Rawfolds Mill and the murder of William Horsfall (April)
Assassination of Spencer Perceval (11 May)
Lord Liverpool becomes Prime Minister (8 June)
Repeal of the Orders in Council
The United States of America declares war on Great Britain
1814 Napoleon exiled to Elba
Liverpool is invested as a Knight of the Garter
Princess Caroline leaves for the continent
The Peace of Ghent ends the war between Britain and the United States (December)
1815 Corn Bill riots (March)
Corn Law prohibits the importation of foreign corn until British corn has reached the price of 80s. (£4) a quarter
Napoleon returns from Elba but is defeated at Waterloo (18 June) and abdicates

1816 Income Tax repealed despite the government's efforts to retain it
Ely and Littleport riots (22–5 May)
Spa Fields riot (December)
1817 Mobbing of the Prince Regent's coach (28 January)
Habeas Corpus suspended (February)
Act against Seditious Meetings (March)
March of the Blanketeers begins (10 March)
Huddersfield Rising (8 June)
Pentrich Rising (9 June)
1818 Peel gives up his office as Chief Secretary for Ireland
1819 Bullion Committee chaired by Peel recommends the phased resumption of cash payments by the Bank of England (May)
'Peterloo' massacre (16 August)
The Six Acts passed to strengthen public order
The Factory Act prohibits children under the age of nine from working in cotton mills, whilst those over nine are restricted to a twelve-hour day
1820 Agricultural depression sets in (reaching its lowest point in 1822)
Death of George III. Accession of George IV (29 January)
Cato Street Conspiracy revealed (February)
Caroline returns to England (June)
Bill of Pains and Penalties (to deprive Caroline of her title and dissolve her marriage to the King) abandoned by the government after its passage through the Lords (10 November)
Canning resigns from the cabinet (December)
1821 Return to the gold standard recommended (May)
Peel declines the office of President of the Board of Control
The King rejects Liverpool's advice to appoint Canning First Lord of the Admiralty
'Carol-loo' riots over the route of Queen Caroline's funeral procession (14 August)
Sidmouth resigns the office of Home Secretary and the Grenville connection joins the government (December)
1822 Peel appointed Home Secretary
Castlereagh commits suicide (12 August)

Canning appointed Foreign Secretary and Leader of the House of Commons

1823 Robinson appointed Chancellor of the Exchequer (January)

Reciprocity of Duties Act facilitates bilateral tariff reductions

Peel begins his revision of the criminal code and reform of the prison system

Huskisson appointed President of the Board of Trade (October)

1824 Hume successfully moves resolutions in the Commons for a committee to consider the law relating to combinations (February)

Repeal of the Combination Laws (June)

1825 Amending Act partially restricts the freedoms arising from the repeal of the Combination Laws, following a wave of strikes

Juries Regulation Act consolidates the laws relating to juries and redefines the qualifications and responsibilities of jury service

A poor harvest results in the average price of wheat rising to its highest point since 1819. The government responds with the Bonded Corn Act which authorises the immediate release of bonded wheat for the home market and the admission of further quantities of grain, if required

Year ends with a banking crisis

1826 Banking Act legalises joint-stock banks outside a 65-mile radius of London

1827 Liverpool suffers a stroke (17 February) and resigns

Canning becomes Prime Minister and Chancellor of the Exchequer (April)

Half of Liverpool's Cabinet (including Wellington and Peel) refuses to serve under Canning

Death of Canning (8 August)

Goderich becomes Prime Minister

1828 Wellington becomes Prime Minister (January)

Death of Liverpool (4 December).

1

Introduction

Amongst their more public vices, politicians are notorious body-snatchers. That is to say, they are apt to appropriate the memory of some great statesman of the past in an attempt to legitimise some contemporary policy or at least enhance their own image by association. Notorious examples of this practice include Disraeli's assumption of the mantle of Palmerston, Lord Randolph Churchill's abduction of the memory of Disraeli, and Margaret Thatcher's attempt to conflate her image with that of Winston Churchill.

On the face of it, Lord Liverpool would appear to be a strong contender for such treatment. After all few, if any, Prime Ministers have such a good claim to have been distinguished leaders of their country in both war and peacetime. Aberdeen, Asquith and Chamberlain, for example, appeared, at least in the judgment of their contemporaries, to have failed the test of war, whilst Lloyd George's and Churchill's finest hours as premiers were clearly confined to their wartime tenures of No. 10.

Moreover, Liverpool's record of fifteen consecutive years of service in the highest office of state has not been surpassed since it was set in 1827 (although Margaret Thatcher came close between 1979 and 1990).

How, then, is one to account for the paradox between Liverpool's political longevity on the one hand, and his rela-

1

tively poor press amongst historians and lowly place amongst party-political hagiographers on the other?

In part, the answer lies in the fact that Liverpool's political career was passed in its entirety, unlike that of, say, Peel, in the unreformed parliament whose assumptions, mechanics and imperatives are even more difficult to comprehend than the political world of the post–1832 period. In part, also, it lies in Liverpool's rather self-effacing character, which whilst admirable in many respects certainly lacked the panache of a Palmerston or Disraeli or even the glamour mustered by a Rosebery or an Eden. He also lacked what Denis Healey called a 'hinterland'. That is to say, with the exception of an appreciation of literature and the fine arts, he had few interests outside the world of politics.

Thus, if one were simultaneously to give hostages to fortune and indulge in a little historical body-snatching of one's own, perhaps the closest figure to that of Liverpool as Prime Minister is not Margaret Thatcher but Clement Attlee, who managed to combine solid legislative achievement with a rather deceptive two-dimensional political personality.

This work will endeavour to justify a sympathetic reassessment of Liverpool's record as party leader and as Prime Minister. In so doing it is hoped that light will be shed on three key questions regarding the period of Liverpool's premiership.

First, what factors combined to produce public disorder between 1812 and 1821? Second, how severe was governmental suppression of that disorder? Third, is it valid to distinguish between 'repressive' and 'liberal' phases of the administration, with the personnel changes centring upon 1822 marking the point of alleged transformation?

There will not be an extended discussion of the nature of party politics in this period or of the early career of Robert Peel or of the period between Liverpool's stroke and the 1832 Reform Act as these matters are dealt with in the relevant sections of three other volumes in the Lancaster Pamphlets series, namely, *Political Parties in Britain 1783–1867*, *Sir Robert Peel: Statesmanship, Power and Party*, and *The Great Reform Act of 1832*, all by Eric J. Evans.

Nor will there be an extended discussion of British foreign policy in this period, except in so far as it is relevant to the questions posed above, as this aspect of Liverpool's administration merits separate treatment.

2

Lord Liverpool, his administration and the problems of Regency England

Spencer Perceval's chief claim to fame is that he is the only British Prime Minister to have been assassinated.

Although the long-standing war with France and serious disturbances within the country might have been a pretext for political assassination, it appears that Perceval's assassin, John Bellingham, was a mentally unbalanced lone gunman, seeking revenge for imprisonment for debt in Russia, rather than part of a conspiracy. Nevertheless, stepping into Perceval's shoes in 1812, given the aforementioned difficulties, was an awesome prospect.

Even though Lord Liverpool was only the Prince Regent's sixth choice as Prime Minister, he was eminently qualified to discharge the difficult task of succeeding Perceval. His father, Charles Jenkinson (1727–1808), had based his career and the family fortune upon a lifetime's devoted service to George III, and had been rewarded with the title of first Baron Hawkesbury in 1786 and first Earl of Liverpool in 1796. After Charterhouse and Christ Church, Oxford, his eldest son, Robert, had first entered Parliament in 1790 (at the age of twenty). His early entry into Parliament enabled him to serve a long political apprenticeship.

After acting as Pitt's Commissioner at the Board of Control (1793), where he developed his knowledge of commercial affairs, and as Master of the Mint (1796), where he had (in the customary manner) augmented his own fortune, he had held the three great secretaryships, having been Foreign Secretary from 1801 to 1803, Home Secretary from 1804 to 1809 (with a brief break in 1806–07) and Secretary for War and Colonies from 1809 to 1812. The last office was arguably of more consequence than the previous two at that stage of the war with France. From 1793 he had never been out of office and from 1801 never out of the cabinet, apart from the short Whig administration of 1806–07.

As Gash has said, 'Few prime ministers have made such a measured ascent to supreme office or been prepared for it by such comprehensive experience'. It is true that James Callaghan held the three great modern offices of Home Secretary, Foreign Secretary and Chancellor of the Exchequer before becoming Prime Minister in 1976, but his ascent to supreme office was not as measured as Liverpool's and he held the premiership for a much shorter period.

In addition to his ministerial appointments, Liverpool had been the Tory Leader in the House of Lords since 1803, where he greatly strengthened the government's debating team against Lord Grenville. Even if few would choose to follow Wellington in placing him on a par with Pitt in this regard, Liverpool was widely acknowledged as a parliamentary speaker of some distinction; one who eschewed orotund rhetoric in favour of closely-reasoned argument. In 1819 his often critical nephew, James Archibald Stuart Wortley (later Baron Wharncliffe), declared his uncle to be perhaps 'the best speaker in either House of Parliament'.

Moreover, Pitt himself had remarked in 1805 that 'with his information . . . and the habits of reflection which he has acquired, he [Liverpool] is by no means a contemptible adviser', although he also said that he was not a man 'to whose decision singly I would commit a great question of policy'. Canning, an altogether more partial witness, had told Pitt that Liverpool possessed 'useful powers of mind, great industry and much information' and later described him to Wellesley as 'an able and honourable man'. In short, Liverpool was regarded as possessing generally sound judgment and a safe pair of hands.

Liverpool was also regarded as a man of high morality in his private and public life. This was an asset which improved with age, as the evangelical revival resulted in rising expectations of exacting moral standards. However, in two respects his scruples had political drawbacks. First, he was so consistently conciliatory and concerned not to cause unnecessary offence to colleagues that anxiety sometimes produced an irritability and depression which threatened to affect his health (although this did not become a serious problem until 1824 when he had to smooth over the differences in cabinet between Canning and his colleagues).

Second, he was too scrupulous to hold out a possibility of patronage which he knew he might not be able to honour. This was a serious disability given that there was insufficient patronage to ensure a reliable government majority in the Commons. Moreover, Liverpool's integrity meant that he was willing to risk making enemies in the highest ranks of society on questions of patronage, as in 1823, when he refused the King's request to make his physician and private secretary, Knighton, a privy councillor, or in 1826, when he refused Wellesley's and Wellington's claims that their younger brother, Gerald, should receive preferment in the Church.

However, in one important respect Liverpool's scrupulous approach did pay dividends. By virtue of the fact that he weighed each question on its merits, he was a High or 'Protestant' Tory in his opposition to Catholic emancipation but was a liberal Tory in his commitment to Free Trade. He was thus ideally placed, by virtue of this intermediate position, to appeal to, and mediate between, the two wings of the Tory party if ever they came into conflict.

Liverpool naturally attempted to balance the two wings of his party in composing his ministry and in his 'inner cabinet' (which consisted of Liverpool, Wellington, Bathurst and Canning after the reconstruction of 1821–3). However, in 1812 Liverpool was unable to secure Canning's services because, although Canning professed himself to be 'sincerely desirous of coming into the Regent's service' and to consider 'a re-union with Liverpool in office as an object . . . most desirable, publickly and privately', he would not take the Foreign Office or the War or Home Departments if his archrival Castlereagh retained the Leadership of the Commons.

The rivalry between the two men went back at least as far as the time when they were cabinet colleagues in the Duke of Portland's ministry of 1807–09. Canning, as Foreign Secretary, had campaigned for Castlereagh's removal from the War Office from March 1809 and had succeeded in this aim in September, following a disastrous military expedition to Walcheren. When Castlereagh resigned the two men fought a duel in which Canning was slightly wounded in his thigh and his pride, whilst Castlereagh lost a coat button after an exchange of two shots apiece. However, in 1812 Castlereagh had already agreed to relinquish the Foreign Office – but not the Leadership of the Commons – to make way for Canning, and thus Liverpool reluctantly felt obliged to refuse Canning's demand.

Thus Castlereagh continued under Liverpool as Foreign Secretary and Leader of the House of Commons and Canning did not enter the administration until 1816, when he temporarily contented himself with the Board of Control, which had become vacant following the death of the Earl of Buckinghamshire.

Shelley famously referred to Liverpool's administration as comprising 'Rulers who neither see, nor feel, nor know', and Disraeli claimed that its members 'knew as little of the real state of their own country as savages of an approaching eclipse'. This harsh judgment has been echoed by several historians. R.J. White, for example, writes that 'By their social intercourse, their classical studies, their mingling in the affairs of county society, and their travels, they could be said to have an extensive knowledge of three things above all else', namely, ancient Rome, modern (non-industrial) England south of the Trent, and those foreign parts which customarily featured on the itinerary of the Grand Tour. Bentley goes even further in suggesting an ignorance of contemporary society when he writes that for most 'the home counties, the southeast and the west country filled their horizons . . . at a moment when the axis of working-class unrest and political radicalism had swung sharply north and west towards centres like Manchester and Glasgow'. Cookson, however, rightly points out that the members of Liverpool's cabinet 'were really less the representatives of the landed aristocracy than professional politicians', like Liverpool's own father, in so far as only one of them, the Earl of Westmorland (the Lord Privy Seal), possessed 'impeccable aristocratic credentials', which came with a long-established title. As the Whig Sir James Graham put it in 1826, it was 'an administration more connected with the annuities than with land, possessed of few acres'.

Castlereagh's roots lay in the substantial Irish gentry. He was the second, but eldest surviving, son of Robert Stewart, who had been ennobled as the first Marquis of Londonderry. Viscount Sidmouth, the Home Secretary, and Vansittart, who belonged to the Sidmouth connection and was Chancellor of the Exchequer, had emerged from the lesser English gentry; Sidmouth, for example, was the son of Dr Anthony Addington, a physician who owned a small estate in Oxfordshire. The Earl of Harrowby, the Lord President of the Council, and Robinson, the Vice-President and then President of the Board of Trade, owed their positions to grandfathers who had prospered in the law and the diplomatic service respectively. Liverpool himself, like Castlereagh and Sidmouth, came from the squirearchy rather than the nobility, for his father had emerged from an Oxfordshire estate bought by the sea-captain and merchant Anthony Jenkinson. It is, however, the career of John Scott, first Earl of Eldon and the Lord Chancellor, which best illustrates the extent to which the world of Regency politics was not monopolised by those of ancient lineage. He was the third son of William Scott, a prosperous coal factor and business man of Newcastle upon Tyne, who had entered the Commons via grammar school, Oxford, marriage to the heiress of a wealthy banker and a distinguished career in the law.

Thus in White's opinion (and offsetting his previously quoted words), 'superimposed upon their landed origins, they possessed the wider outlook and interests of professional politicians', having come to ministerial office, with very few exceptions, 'by the long and arduous road of public service, not by the mere possession of titles and estates'.

Liverpool was certainly not ignorant of the impact of the industrial revolution. In 1824 he recommended Lord Stanhope to visit Britain's new manufacturing towns, praising the steam engine as 'the greatest and most useful invention of modern Times'. He also urged the King to sanction a £500 treasury grant in order to erect a statue of James Watt.

There was, however, one constraint upon Liverpool's government which has been pointed out by Bentley and which was of greater significance than their social origins or regional knowledge, namely, their age. 'Most ministers had been born in the early years of the reign of George III'; Sidmouth and Eldon – aged fifty-five and sixty-one respectively in 1812 – had been born even earlier. In so far as these men lacked insight into the problems of the age, this was because they were children of the eighteenth century attempting to cope with the problems of the nineteenth.

Liverpool took control of a Britain beset by problems of a daunting number and magnitude, which conspired to produce considerable social unrest.

The move towards a more capitalist system of farming was socially destabilising to the extent that it facilitated both rural depopulation and massive population growth, up from 10.5 million in 1801 (the year of the first census) to 12 million in 1811 and 14.1 million in 1821. This in turn meant that much of the population was very young (with an estimated forty-eight per cent of the population of England and Wales below fifteen years of age in 1821). This may also have contributed to popular unrest for it provided protest movements with an abundance of young males.

The argument of the Reverend Thomas Malthus in his 1798 *Essay on Population* that the supply of food increased in accordance with an arithmetic ratio, whilst the number of mouths to be fed increased in accordance with a geometric ratio, heightened alarm in educated circles. According to Malthus, famine threatened if the populace could not be persuaded to exercise moral restraint.

Boyd Hilton writes that 'Malthus's terrifying spectre haunted the ministerial imagination' and Liverpool himself wrote to Sidmouth in 1817 that, 'if our Commercial Situation does not improve, Emigration, or Premature Deaths, are the only Remedies. Both must occur to a considerable Extent. It would be most inhuman in such Case, to encourage the latter, by prohibiting the former.'

The growth of population was perhaps encouraged by the so-called Speenhamland System of poor relief. Named after the Berkshire village where it was first employed, in 1795, this consisted of providing bread or money, out of the local poor rates, to those unemployed or in receipt of a wage considered to be below the subsistence level. Payments were also made proportionate to family size. This system was criticised for encouraging the growth of large families and providing an incentive for unscrupulous employers to underpay their labourers, secure in the knowledge that any deficit would be made up out of local taxation. This then effectively obliged their more scrupulous brethren to follow suit or find themselves less able to compete. Although the Speenhamland system was not universal the poor-rates certainly bore down very heavily upon taxpayers, quadrupling between 1775 and 1817.

Popular unrest was also fuelled by industrialisation. The increasing concentration of potential malcontents was particularly alarming for those in authority.

Moreover, the industrial revolution also brought technological unemployment, as new machinery rendered traditional skills – and skilled workers – redundant. West Riding croppers, Lancashire cotton weavers and Midlands framework knitters were amongst those who turned to machine-breaking, or Luddism, between 1811 and 1817, although in some instances it was not the introduction of new machinery undercutting older forms of craft production which triggered the disturbances; machines were broken simply because this provided the best available means of protesting against other grievances, including wage reductions, the employment of unapprenticed workmen and the production of inferior goods.

In February 1812 the Perceval administration had responded to the Luddite threat – which had been particularly severe in Nottingham – by passing the Framebreaking Act, which made the crime a capital offence, and the Watch and Ward Act, whereby the Nottingham authorities were empowered (until 1 March 1814) to respond to any actual or perceived local threat to the peace by directing that every resident male over the age of seventeen who was paying poor-rates should police their local community.

The failure of this legislation to act as an effective deterrent to Luddite activity was shown most clearly by the events of April 1812, which included an attack on William Cartwright's Rawfolds Mill, during which two Luddites named Hartley and Booth were killed, and the murder of the millowner William Horsfall, for which the Luddites Mellor, Thorpe and Smith were hanged in January 1813.

Luddism was described by E.J. Hobsbawm as a form of 'collective bargaining by riot', and this description makes sense since until the Combination Laws of 1799–1800 were repealed in 1824–5, trade union activity remained illegal. Moreover, there was only limited opportunity for most working men to vote.

The extra-parliamentary agitation for parliamentary reform particularly associated with William Cobbett, Major Cartwright, and Henry 'Orator' Hunt was perceived by those in authority as deriving inspiration from the example of the French Revolution of 1789 and was certainly fuelled by the feeling that the wars with France which had begun in 1793 were unnecessary and had been mismanaged.

The French Revolutionary and Napoleonic Wars, which lasted from 1793 to 1815 (apart from the fourteen-month respite occasioned by the March 1802 Peace of Amiens) were enormously costly and damaging. This was particularly so because of the Continental System: Napoleon's attempt to throttle British trade by means of a blockade which began in November 1806. The Orders in Council of January, November and December 1807 were an attempt to break the blockade by restricting the scope for neutrals to trade with Napoleonic Europe. This not only induced recession but also contributed to the chronic deterioration in Anglo-American relations which ultimately led to the decision of the United States to declare war on Great Britain in June 1812, despite repeal of the Orders in Council in the same month. This war was to last until December 1814, and in fact continued into 1815 since it took time for news of the peace to reach the Americas. As a result of these conflicts the National Debt increased from £238 million in 1793 to £902 million in 1816.

Liverpool was also beset by political difficulties. The Tory party, which in the Commons comprised only slightly more than a quarter of all MPs, was a coalition divided in its attitude to the question of Catholic emancipation, and Liverpool had only succeeded in forming his administration in 1812 by allowing this to remain an open question: a condition insisted upon by the Prince Regent.

Moreover, Liverpool could only govern the country if he retained the confidence and goodwill of not only the Prince Regent but also of the large number of MPs who were not committed to one of the political parties.

The opportunities for patronage had declined whilst the modern machinery of party management had not yet evolved, rendering Liverpool more dependent than either his predecessors or successors upon the goodwill of an exceptionally independent-minded House of Commons. As Charles Arbuthnot, the Joint Secretary of the Treasury, complained to Castlereagh in 1819, 'with all our sweeping reductions of patronage, I have not the tie I once had upon the independent members'.

It also so happened that the prestige of the monarchy was probably at an all-time low during this period, given George III's 'madness' (now thought to have been due to porphyria) and the Prince Regent's extravagance and scandalous private life, notably his attempted suicide and secret marriage with the twice-widowed Catholic Mrs Fitzherbert in 1785. The Prince resented his marriage of 1795 to the coarse Princess Caroline of Brunswick, with the result that they had separated in 1796, had set up rival households and had both engaged in numerous indiscreet liaisons.

After George became Prince Regent in February 1811, following a relapse into incoherence by his father, he was to make Liverpool's position extraordinarily difficult by virtue of his clear personal dislike of the ministry, disputes over patronage (for example, over Liverpool's aforementioned reluctance to make Sir William Knighton, the King's favourite, a privy councillor) and royal expenditure (notably those costs arising from the extensive alterations and rebuilding in St James's Park, Buckingham House and Windsor Castle), and the Queen Caroline affair of 1820–21, when he sought to deprive his wife of her claims as Queen.

The Civil List was a source of embarrassment for the government, particularly when times were hard, for 'no subject is viewed with more jealousy and suspicion', the Prince Regent was warned by Liverpool's government, 'than the personal expenses of the Sovereign or his representative at a time when most of the landed gentlemen of the country are obliged to submit to losses & privations as well as to retrenchment'. And Huskisson, a key adviser of Liverpool's on economic affairs, warned Canning in 1816 that 'Upon this subject we are forewarned not to expect the support of many who are generally our friends in the House; and out of doors public opinion is still more decidedly against us.'

Moreover, by 1812 no fewer than nine of the cabinet – including Liverpool himself, of course – sat in the House of Lords and the ministerial team in the Commons lacked debating strength. Castlereagh, Vansittart, and Bragge-Bathurst (the Chancellor of the Duchy of Lancaster) were simply no match for Whigs and radicals such as Brougham, Tierney, Mackintosh, Romilly, Hume and Burdett, particularly when Castlereagh was engaged in lengthy diplomatic negotiations abroad. Liverpool wistfully expressed the hope that 'a second Pitt' might emerge from amongst 'the most promising of the young men' in the Commons, such as Palmerston (Secretary at War), Peel (Chief Secretary for Ireland), Robinson and Huskisson (First Commissioner of Woods and Forests from 1814).

On the face of it, the coming of peace might have been expected to relieve the government's difficulties, not least since Liverpool could claim credit for having won the war. On the contrary, the end of the wars with France and the United States excited expectations which could not be fulfilled and removed 'a centripetal force in a society which had become increasingly subject to the centrifugal forces of an industrial revolution', in the words of White.

Peace released those energies which had been harnessed by the war and, as Cookson puts it, 'the greater the effort and therefore derangement of war the greater the pangs of peacetime recovery'. Liverpool wrote to Castlereagh that 'the country at this moment is peace mad. Many of our best friends think of nothing but reduction of taxes and low establishments'.

Certainly, the transition from wartime to peacetime conditions accentuated, where it did not actually create, economic difficulties. Adjustments had to be made in line with the reduced demand for products associated with the war effort, including provisions, clothing, timber, iron, leather, canvas and rope. Moreover, rapid demobilisation put nearly a third of a million ex-servicemen on the already glutted labour market. This depressed wage levels, added to unemployment, increased the burden of local taxation and – what was potentially most dangerous – ensured that the discontented would be led by those with military experience.

Furthermore, with the coming of peace the landed interest – or at least that part of it which had taken advantage of inflated wartime prices to cultivate marginal land – feared that their investment would be wiped out and agriculture undermined by an influx of cheap foreign corn if they were not protected. They argued that a Corn Law was justified in the interests of national security, as Britain might once again need to maximise the domestic supply of foodstuffs to counteract the effects of blockade, and in the interests of domestic stability, as agriculture was the single largest employer of labour and was already subject to rural depopulation.

Mindful of his fragile position and genuinely wishing to canvass opinion, Liverpool called two very full meetings (on 11 and 14 February 1815) of those, on both sides of the House, interested in discussing the proposed Corn Law. Moreover, despite having expressed its own preference for the sliding scale proposed by Huskisson and supported by Liverpool, the government took the extraordinary step of allowing those present to decide the final nature of the proposed legislation, with the result that free importation was only permitted once home-produced corn had reached the price of 80 shillings (£4) a quarter. This decision was in line with the recommendation of an 1814 committee on the issue and the preferences of both Robinson, who was to pilot the bill through the Commons, and C.C. Western, the Whig member for Essex, who was widely regarded as the spokesman of the agricultural interest. This decision – together with bad harvests – helped to ensure that the average price of corn, which provided the staple element in the British working-class diet, was higher in the years 1810–19 than at any other time during the whole of the nineteenth century.

The Corn Law of 1815 was certainly open to attack on the grounds that it caused unnecessary suffering for the already hard-pressed working classes by artificially raising the price of their bread simply in order to maintain the artificially high profits of the landed interest, who comprised the country's lawmakers. It also damaged industry to the extent that it made the manufacturers' wages bill unnecessarily high and hindered international trade. In short, it could be regarded as selfish class legislation which ran counter to the national interest and the new ideas of free trade, and which merely encouraged inefficiency and greed.

Hence the Corn Bill riots of March 1815 during which special constables were enrolled, 1,300 infantry and cavalry were stationed in the capital and the Life Guards charged the London crowd with drawn sabres. Hence, too, a number of food riots in the provinces, of which the most famous took place in Ely and Littleport between 22 and 25 May 1816, under the slogan of 'Bread or Blood'. One of the rioters was killed during the suppression of the disorders and at the Special Assize for the Isle of Ely, where the captured were put on trial for their lives, twenty-four were convicted, of whom five were executed whilst the others were sentenced to transportation or imprisonment.

William Hobhouse, a Treasury solicitor who helped to prepare the case for the prosecution, clearly viewed the proceedings as serving a deterrent purpose, for he wrote to Beckett at the Home Office that 'the Convictions of yesterday have had a very salutary effect' and expressed the hope 'that the general result of the Commission will entirely bring about the Effect which it was the object of the Government to produce'.

The prosecution had alleged a conspiracy, although the Keeper of Bury St Edmunds Gaol, where many of the accused were imprisoned, stated that he felt 'assured that none of these outrages have happened from any organised system but from the great dissatisfaction . . . and the want of employ'. His analysis was supported by the Board of Agriculture Report for 1816 which said that 'The state of the labouring poor is very deplorable and arises entirely from want of employment, which they are willing to seek, but the farmer cannot furnish'. However, instead of attempting to tackle this problem, the government took the easier option of addressing one of its symptoms and passed the Game Act in 1816, which increased the penalty for poaching from one month's hard labour to seven years' transportation. In the event, such was the extent of agrarian distress that this recourse to stiffer sentences did little or nothing to deter the crime.

In 1816 moreover, the government failed, by thirty-seven votes, to win parliamentary support for its plan to retain the income tax which had been introduced in 1797 as a wartime exigency, and chose not to renew the war excise on malt. Together these levies produced £17.5 million per annum or about a quarter of the government's revenue. Their disappearance 'grievously disrupted the transition to peace' according to Boyd Hilton, by postponing the return to the gold standard (whereby paper currency was backed by bullion), and ultimately led to additional taxation on articles of general consumption, which bore down disproportionately hard on the already hard-pressed poor. As Liverpool wrote to Canning, 'Those who raise this Clamour [to remove the income tax] have a Narrow View of their own Interest' given that the restoration of public credit, and consequent fall in interest rates would 'afford more Relief to the existing Distresses of the Country, than any other Measure which could be adopted'.

Since it was not initially considered politically feasible to raid the Sinking Fund or introduce new taxes, the only alternative was increased borrowing. However, the National Debt had already increased from £238 million in 1793 to £902 million in 1816 and roughly eighty per cent of government expenditure was required merely to pay the interest on the sum borrowed.

More fundamentally, the failure to retain the income tax obliged the government to postpone its overhaul of the tax structure, as the immediate need to meet the shortfall in projected revenue reduced the scope for freeing trade by the reduction or abolition of duties.

This parliamentary failure was symptomatic of the political weaknesses of Liverpool's government that have already been noted, namely, its lack of patronage, absence of any machinery for enforcing party discipline, and weakness in terms of debating talent on the front bench in the Commons. Political expediency thus combined with personal regard to ensure that Liverpool repeatedly risked disfavour with his cabinet colleagues and the Prince Regent in order to bolster his ministry's front bench in the Commons by securing Canning's services.

Liverpool and Canning had been nicknamed 'the inseparables' from their time together at Christ Church, Oxford, and the two men were always close, despite Liverpool's being moved to tears on at least one occasion by Canning's sarcasm towards him. Liverpool nevertheless valued Canning's talents highly and overlooked his defects more willingly than most men; he had been genuinely disappointed that Canning had not entered the ministry in 1812.

Liverpool did everything within his power to keep his lines of communication with Canning open: manoeuvring in vain for Canning to replace Viscount Melville as First Lord of the Admiralty in 1813 and inviting Canning to undertake an embassy to Portugal in 1814. Privately, Liverpool promised Canning the first available cabinet vacancy.

Whatever talents had been available to the government it would, however, have been difficult for them to counter the arguments of the regular Whig opposition MPs, some one hundred and fifty strong. The opposition rallied under the popular and traditional banner of retrenchment, claiming that the end of the war allowed economy and implying that continued extravagance suggested tyrannical designs by the executive. Notwithstanding the government's programme of rapid demobilisation, the Whigs focused on the desirability of reducing the size of the standing army on the grounds that, in the government's own words, the treaties concluded at Paris guaranteed a lasting peace, whilst the navy represented the first line of defence in the event of war. They presented a large standing army as a standing invitation to meddle in continental affairs or threaten domestic liberties.

The government was thus forced into the embarrassing position of trimming another £340,000 off the army estimates in the spring of 1816, after having claimed that they had previously been pared to the bone. Huskisson's verdict on the affair was that the concession came 'rather awkwardly after the general assurance in the Speech that the utmost economy had been attended to in all the Estimates'.

It was, however, the threat to Liverpool's administration and to the ruling class in general from outside parliament which has chiefly exercised historians of the period.

3
Disorder and reaction, 1811–17

There is a vast literature on revolutions, which considers the phenomenon both in the abstract and in its historical manifestations. This literature is of little or no value in determining the extent to which Regency Britain was close to revolution. Nevertheless, a few general points may be made before looking at the period in more detail.

The examination of successful revolutions suggests that for a revolution to succeed four processes must first take place. These four preconditions are: the delegitimation of the existing regime; the legitimation of the revolutionary position; the construction of a force outside the control of the state, and subversion of the state's forces.

The process of denying the title to authority of the existing regime is a relatively easy one given that it is a purely negative intellectual exercise and that the deficiencies and drawbacks of a given state, such as the taxation which it levies, are usually much more visible and keenly felt than its advantages. It should, however, be noted that alienation must be so complete that the putative revolutionary rejects not merely the government of the day but the regime in its entirety.

The process of legitimating one's own revolutionary position is, of course, the mirror-image of delegitimating existing authority, and religion and other ideologies used to sanctify the status quo can be turned, with relative ease, into the means of questioning that same state of affairs.

The construction of a force outside the control of the state is more difficult than the processes mentioned above but is not as difficult as it might appear to be at first sight because of the international dimension. That is to say, it is often possible for would be revolutionaries to gain practical assistance from some foreign power in subverting the state.

This may occur for ideological reasons but is more usually motivated by strategic or geopolitical considerations. Examples of such assistance include the aid given by the French, Dutch and Spanish to the American colonists rebelling against British rule during the American War of Independence (1775–83) and that given by the German High Command to Lenin in 1917.

If a foreign power does not assist revolutionaries directly it may assist them indirectly by means of successful warfare with the state which the revolutionaries seek to undermine, as defeat not only demoralises the armed guardians of the regime but undermines any regime's pretensions to legitimacy insofar as it is thereby shown to have failed in its primary function of protecting its citizens from foreign invasion. For example, the Japanese assisted the Russian revolutionaries in this manner in 1905. However, the ultimate failure of the 1905 Revolution in Russia because the army remained loyal to the Czar suggests that the subversion of the state's armed forces is the last and most difficult of these processes for revolutionaries to achieve.

If one accepts the above as the preconditions necessary for revolution it is possible to say that the prospects for success during Liverpool's premiership were not good. The French Revolution clearly provided the means of delegitimating the existing regime and legitimating the revolutionary position, and some radicals clearly sought to copy the tactics and borrow the symbols of their French counterparts. Thus the Spencean insurrectionists at Spa Fields in December 1816 spoke of setting up a Committee of Public Safety and paraded the red, white and green tricolour of the future British Republic. However, what is more remarkable is the way in which most critics of the status quo preferred to speak in traditional terms of the 'ancient constitution' and the supposedly concrete civil, customary or conventional rights due to a 'freeborn Englishman' rather than adopt the abstract philosophical language of the Rights of

Man which had become common currency across the Channel. According to Dinwiddy even London's far left preferred to embrace 'a bizarre mixture of Saxon constitutionalism, seventeenth-century republicanism, agrarian socialism, pseudo-religious millenarianism, and sheer saturnalian ribaldry' rather than jacobinism.

Moreover, when Britain emerged as the victor at the end of the wars with France this not only enhanced the prestige of the regime, notwithstanding the problems brought by peace, but also deprived potential revolutionaries of their only real chance of outside assistance in constructing a force outside state control. The threat of revolution in Britain was thus greatly diminished by 1815.

Last but not least, although there was much discontent amongst the demobilised, the armed forces remained loyal. The only suspicion of disloyalty on their part occurred – as will be shown – during the Queen Caroline affair which, by its very nature, shows that delegitimation of existing forms of authority had not progressed very far.

Having established that the threat of revolution in Britain was not great, one should of course remember that contemporaries were not in a position to view affairs with such equanimity. The French Revolution of 1789 bred a form of hysteria, and the spectre of jacobinism haunted the ruling classes of late eighteenth- and early nineteenth-century Europe in a far more immediate manner than the fear of over-population. The nature of the perceived threat of revolution in Britain and the reaction of the authorities will now be examined in more detail.

British working-class interest in politics of a radical character was certainly reflected in, and stimulated, by the spread of Major Cartwright's Hampden Clubs, the popularity of William Cobbett's unstamped (and therefore relatively cheap) *Political Register*, first issued in November 1816, and Henry 'Orator' Hunt's platform campaigning. None of these leaders of popular radicalism could, however, be described as a typical horny-handed son of toil and none of them was a denizen of the new industrial towns north of the Trent. Indeed, one could plausibly argue that the landowners who dominated Liverpool's cabinet had a far more extensive knowledge of the country which they governed than did their leading critics outside parliament.

Henry Hunt was born in Wiltshire in 1773 and inherited

3,000 acres in his home county as well as property in Bath and Somerset, including the manor and estate of Glastonbury. His transition from prosperous gentleman farmer and loyal member of the local yeomanry to radical demagogue owed much to his ostracism from county society. This in turn arose from both envy of his success and disapproval of his behaviour, notably his separation from his wife and elopement with an unhappily-married woman.

John Cartwright had been born into an old Northamptonshire landed family in 1740, and after a distinguished career in the navy had begun his public involvement in politics in 1775 by expressing himself in favour of American independence. It was also in this year that he was appointed a major in the Nottinghamshire militia and expressed himself in favour of the radical reform of parliament, including universal suffrage, the secret ballot and annual parliaments.

Cartwright thus combined a respectable background with the possession of extremely radical views, so that he was viewed as a class traitor by some and as a persecuted champion of the oppressed by others, following the cancellation of his commission and his conviction for sedition in 1820.

Cartwright died in 1824 but he left a legacy of roughly eighty political tracts and a string of about one hundred and fifty Hampden Clubs (named after the seventeenth-century Buckinghamshire squire who had resisted the arbitrary imposition of ship money during the so-called Personal Rule of Charles I), which provided a network for the propagation of a range of radical ideas, symbolised by the convention of Hampden Club delegates which was held in London in January 1817.

In contrast, William Cobbett was born of peasant stock in 1762. He entered political journalism in the United States after a variety of employments (including eight years of service in a regiment of the line). In 1800 he returned to Britain and by 1804 had turned his back on his earlier Tory politics and come out in favour of the cause of reform, most notably through his *Political Register*, which ran almost continuously from January 1802 until his death in 1835. Its circulation and influence were greatly enhanced in late 1816, when Cobbett reduced its price to twopence by evading the stamp duty.

It was Cobbett who said 'I defy you to agitate a man on a full stomach', thereby implying that economic hardship was an essential precondition of popular unrest. Liverpool made a similar remark in October 1816 when, in a letter to Sidmouth, he blamed the forthcoming 'Stormy Winter' on 'the evil of a high Price of Bread coming upon us before we have got rid of our Commercial and Agricultural Distresses'.

This point was also borne out by the fact that some rioters apparently believed that the provisional government for which they agitated was so named because it would ensure a more abundant supply of provisions.

Several historians – including W.W. Rostow, T.S. Ashton and E.J. Hobsbawm – have taken the view that economic hardship certainly underlay the popular unrest of early nineteenth-century Britain. Rostow, most famously, produced a 'social tension' chart, showing the movement of wheat prices and the fluctuations of the trade cycle between 1790 and 1850, which appeared to demonstrate that the peaks of popular disturbances coincided with those periods of greatest economic difficulty for the working classes – in 1795, 1800, 1812, 1819, 1830–31, 1839, 1842 and 1848.

However, E.P. Thompson attacked such 'gross economic reductionism', or 'economism' and wrote that class consciousness 'arises in the same way in different times and places, but never in just the same way' and it is certainly the case that the unrest which occurred during Liverpool's administration was confined to particular places rather than affecting the entire nation. This is hardly surprising given not only the relatively primitive nature of communications but also the fact that whilst groups such as the framework-knitters of the east Midlands out-villages and the agricultural labourers suffered a sharp decline in terms of both status and income in the post-war period, other sections of the working class benefited from the fall in the general price level and consequent rise in average real incomes.

Indeed, protest often occurred not, as Rostow would suggest, at the time of greatest hardship but rather when there was a setback to an improving or static situation. Thus the key factor was often a perception of 'relative deprivation' rather than any absolute deterioration in conditions: a phenomenon known as the Davies 'J–curve', after the graphic representation of the relationship between economic development and actual and anticipated satisfaction of needs first formulated by James C. Davies.

It was this element of perceived injustice which was the decisive factor in mobilising attacks against 'unfair' machines or work practices, rather than any imported ideology of revolution, notwithstanding Liverpool's lament that 'the French Revolution had . . . directed the attention of the lower Orders of the Community, and those immediately above them to Political Considerations' and had 'shaken all respect for established authority and antient Institutions'.

It is true that Luddism resulted in great destruction of property, with almost 1,000 frames, worth over £6,000, destroyed in 1811 alone. Hence Perceval's government reacted by imposing the death penalty for machine-breaking and eventually 12,000 troops – almost half the size of the peacetime garrison and a larger body of men than Wellington had taken to Portugal in 1808 – were stationed in the disturbed areas. However, this should not lead historians to exaggerate the extent of the threat.

Luddism was a very restricted movement in both occupational and geographical terms, and was almost always directed against the property rather than the persons of their enemies. The Horsfall case was exceptional. Certainly more blood was shed in suppressing Luddism than was shed by the Luddites themselves.

Similarly, despite the labourers' threatening slogan 'Bread or Blood', the authorities shed more blood than the rioting agricultural labourers of 1816, whose unrest was centred upon the fenlands and came to an end with the return of good harvests and the example set by the Special Assize.

On the face of it, the Spa Fields riot of December 1816 appears to have been a much more ominous development. Unlike the Corn Bill riots of the previous year, this threat to the capital clearly involved genuine revolutionaries. However, once the background and nature of the riot have been studied, the threat can be more realistically evaluated as negligible.

The organising committee which planned a public meeting of the 'Distressed Manufacturers, Mariners, Artisans, and others, of the Cities of London and Westminster, the Borough of Southwark, and the parts adjacent, at Spa Fields' for 15 November 1816 were members of the tiny Society of Spencean Philanthropists, including its Secretary, the lame shoemaker Thomas Preston, the ex-lieutenant in the militia and failed farmer Arthur

Thistlewood, and Dr James Watson and his son, also named James, who were both surgeons or apothecaries.

As followers of the radical Thomas Spence (1750–1814) they sought fundamental changes in society, centring upon nationalisation of the land, and some of their number naively believed that the country would rise up in revolution if they were to provide a lead.

Hunt, unlike Cobbett, accepted the invitation to speak at this first Spa Fields meeting in support of the presentation of 'a memorial to the Prince Regent, setting forth their grievances, and praying for relief'. Hunt, helped by Cobbett, also drew up resolutions and an address for the meeting which scrupulously kept within the law.

It is true that Hunt's programme of universal suffrage was more radical than the direct-taxation suffrage which was the declared programme of the Hampden Club convention, which was due to assemble in January 1817. However, Hunt appeared to have drawn the sting from the Spencean would-be insurrectionists with his plan for a national campaign of open mass meetings, modelled on the first Spa Fields meeting, which was attended by between 5,000 and 15,000 people and which passed off peacefully. The more hot-headed Spenceans, such as Thistlewood and the younger James Watson, therefore decided to hijack the second Spa Fields meeting of 2 December, which had been called to receive the Prince Regent's response to their petition with its 24,479 signatures.

The large crowd that assembled to hear Hunt was incited by the Spenceans to attack prisons, the Bank of England and the Tower of London in an obvious imitation of the storming of the Bastille. A splinter group of several hundred broke away from the orderly main body of the meeting which peaceably waited to hear Hunt. Gunsmiths' shops were ransacked. A customer at one was shot in the groin when he tried to remonstrate with the younger Watson, and a boy was shot in the face in the course of the looting of a butcher's shop. Strong ale and the prospect of loot, rather than strong words and the prospect of liberty, appear to have motivated most of those who participated. Spenceans like Thistlewood cannot be accused of being mere armchair revolutionaries but nevertheless they were essentially taproom politicians engaged in the vain pursuit of pipedreams.

The authorities suppressed this unrest with ease, not least

because they had been kept well-informed by the spy John Castle who had infiltrated the Spencean Society, and because the loyalty of the troops was never in question. Thus Peel (who at this stage was Irish Chief Secretary) was right to dismiss Spa Fields as 'trumpery proceedings' and to protest against magnifying 'a mob into rebellion'.

Nevertheless, the authorities attempted to prosecute Thistlewood, Dr Watson, and three others on charges of high treason. They were acquitted in June 1817, or, to be more precise, the Crown declined to produce further evidence after the jury found Watson 'Not Guilty'.

In the meantime however, another act of unruliness by the London mob forced the government into taking legislative steps to curb unrest, for at the State Opening of Parliament, on 28 January 1817, the Prince Regent's coach was mobbed and one of its windowpanes was broken. Liverpool's government, which needed to retain George's confidence, had to make some gesture to appease royal indignation when the brickbats hurled in his direction assumed physical form and were so well-aimed.

Cookson claims that it was the Spa Fields riot of December 1816 and not the attack on the Prince Regent of January 1817 which was decisive in persuading the government to take emergency powers but to speak of an 'emergency' when almost four months had been allowed to lapse before those powers were acquired is surely sufficient to discredit this interpretation.

After secret committees of both Houses of Parliament had considered the evidence of organised sedition, the government passed several acts which its critics view as reactionary. However, the terms and operation of these acts can be used to support the view that it acted with remarkable moderation.

The mobbing of the Prince Regent's coach had made the government realise that he was not protected under the terms of the Treasonable and Seditious Practices Act of 1795, so it was natural that the government should turn its attention to a range of measures which might prevent repetition of any such disorders.

The suspension of Habeas Corpus (whereby those placed under arrest have to be brought to trial) in February 1817 was, however, temporary and partial, as it only allowed for the imprisonment without trial of those arrested for treason or on suspicion of treason.

24

In fact only forty-four were arrested on suspicion of treason, of whom thirty-seven were detained. One of these was released soon after, whilst a second was discharged on compassionate grounds, and a third died in custody. The remaining thirty-four, committed on sworn evidence to detention, had all been released by the time Habeas Corpus was fully restored in January 1818.

As Gash remarks, 'It was not exactly a reign of terror', and E.P. Thompson must have employed the word 'many' very loosely if one is to accept his claim that 'throughout 1817 many reformers remained imprisoned under the suspension of Habeas Corpus'.

The Seditious Meetings Act of March 1817 was of similarly brief duration and similarly moderate. It laid down that, with certain exceptions, meetings of fifty or more could not take place until permission had been granted by a magistrate. Under its terms meetings like that of December 1816 at Spa Fields could no longer take place.

Moreover, the avowedly subversive Spencean societies were proscribed, a system of licensing of 'every House, Room, Field, or other Place' used for public debate or lecture was instituted, and the death penalty was imposed for incitement of members of the armed forces to mutiny.

Numerous distressed cotton weavers who realised that the law had temporarily deprived them of the ability to congregate in large numbers decided to march in small groups from St Peter's Fields, Manchester to London. They were equipped with blankets, provisions and petitions, and set out on their journey on 10 March 1817 with the intention of presenting their case to the Prince Regent.

As long as these 'Blanketeers' committed no riot or trespass and caused no obstruction or breach of the peace, it was difficult to see how they might lawfully be prevented from completing their journey, despite the fact that this hunger march might come to resemble the 'Bread March of the Women' to Versailles of 5 October 1789 by its end. The authorities certainly took no chances and, ignoring the legal niceties, ensured that the march was broken up.

The next case of unrest was superficially more ominous, for on 8–9 June 1817 several hundred men engaged in uprisings which they (mistakenly) believed to be part of a national insurrection.

25

The Huddersfield rising of 8 June saw a few hundred men who had gathered on the surrounding moors in preparation for a march upon Huddersfield flee upon the approach of the yeomanry and a few constables. Those arrested were acquitted by a jury of charges of burglary.

The Derbyshire rising or Pentrich rebellion of 9 June, which comprises the inspiration and centrepiece of R.J. White's *Waterloo to Peterloo*, is better known but was a similar fiasco, in which perhaps as many as three hundred labourers, quarrymen, ironworkers, and stocking-makers set out, some under duress, from villages like Pentrich at the foot of the Derbyshire Peak, armed with a few guns, pikes and scythes, to seize Nottingham Castle, proclaim a provisional government, rally the Midlands, cross the Trent and march on London. In fact they got no further than shooting a farm servant through a kitchen window as he pulled on his boots.

It is still a matter of historical dispute whether W.J. Richards ('Oliver the Spy') acted as an *agent provocateur* or merely as a paid informer. Either way, the Nottingham magistrates had been aware of the plot since 23 May and the rising was therefore easily suppressed by the men of the 15th Hussars. Isaac Ludlam, William Turner, and the charismatic ringleader Jeremiah Brandreth were found guilty of high treason and were executed on 7 November 1817.

These episodes have been eagerly seized upon by historians either to argue that the potential for a genuinely working-class national insurrection existed or, conversely, to show that violent unrest was the work of a handful of gullible hotheads who were whipped up by *agents provocateurs* before being strung up by the authorities.

E.P. Thompson, for example, criticised the latter view and claimed that the Pentrich rising should be seen as 'one of the first attempts in history to mount a wholly proletarian insurrection' so that even 'without Oliver's patent provocations, some kind of insurrection would probably have been attempted, and perhaps with a greater measure of success'.

In fact the Huddersfield and Pentrich risings, like the other disturbances of 1811–17, posed no significant threat to the authorities, so that even Thompson was forced to concede that the story of the Pentrich rising 'illustrates the weakness of the revolutionary organisation, and the lack of an experienced leadership'. The revelation of the activities of 'Oliver the Spy' and the 'martyrdom' of the rebels merely provided radical critics of the government with much useful propaganda. The Manchester magistrates were soon to make the mistake of creating martyrs on an even grander scale.

4

Disorder and reaction, 1818–21

Precisely because the threats posed by the Blanketeers and the Huddersfield and Pentrich rebels were negligible when coolly considered by the government, because prosperity was returning, and because they had no wish to be seen to be clinging to emergency powers, Liverpool's government allowed the suspension of Habeas Corpus and the Seditious Meetings Act to lapse in 1818. Hunt duly resumed his campaign of mass open-air meetings, designed to impress government with the extent of popular support for parliamentary reform.

On 16 August 1819 a crowd estimated at about 60,000 assembled in St Peter's Fields, Manchester in the hope of at least catching sight of Hunt's famous white top hat. However, the Manchester authorities were needlessly alarmed at this prospect, despite the efforts of Liverpool's government to calm their fears. On 4 August the Home Office had informed the Manchester authorities that reflection had convinced Sidmouth 'the more strongly of the inexpediency of attempting forcibly to prevent the meeting'. The Home Secretary, the missive continued, was of the opinion that unless the mob proceeded to acts of felony or riot, it would be the wisest course of action to abstain from any attempt at dispersal, even if a representative was elected or sedition uttered.

This wise counsel was, however, ignored, as the Manchester magistrates sent fifty men of the Manchester and Salford yeomanry – an imperfectly trained volunteer cavalry force – into the multitudes to arrest Hunt. When they became engulfed the regulars of the 15th Hussars were sent in to rescue them.

John Tyas, who had been detailed to cover the meeting by *The Times*, and who had secured a vantage point on Hunt's waggon, reported that as soon as Hunt had jumped down, 'a cry was made by the cavalry, "Have at their flags."' which resulted in their attempting to seize not only the flags which were in the waggon, but also those which were posted among the crowd, so that they used their sabres indiscriminately in order to get at them, and thereby stampeded the crowd.

The colours of the tricolours thus acted like the proverbial red rag to the mounted representatives of John Bull, with the net result that eleven were killed and a number usually estimated at four hundred, including women and children, were injured.

The government's response to these events was insensitive. The Crown law advisers confirmed the legality of the Manchester authorities' actions and Hunt and three others were tried and convicted of unlawful and seditious assembly. The government pointed out that a third of the casualties were 'self-inflicted' because caused by stampede rather than by sabre and Liverpool and Sidmouth added insult to injury by applauding the magistracy and the military for 'their prompt, decisive and efficient measures for the preservation of the public tranquility'.

In common discourse, by contrast, the incident was labelled 'Peterloo', or the Peterloo massacre, in ironic reference to the battle of Waterloo which had taken place just over four years previously. This sarcasm had added resonance given that the victor of Waterloo, the Duke of Wellington, who was identified with the policy of reaction, had entered Liverpool's cabinet as Master-General of the Ordnance in 1818 and that one of the victims of St Peter's Fields, John Lees, who died of a sabre wound three weeks after Peterloo, was also a veteran of Waterloo.

Peterloo was taken up by the Whigs in September 1819 when Earl Grey suggested that they should sponsor county meetings in order to depict the actions of the Manchester magistrates and the approval of those actions by the government as a threat to constitutional liberties. It was hoped that in tandem with criticism of radical firebrands like Hunt, this policy might attract support to the Whigs at the expense of both the Tories and the radicals.

It was in pursuit of this policy that William, second Earl Fitzwilliam in the English peerage, and Lord Lieutenant of the West Riding of Yorkshire, gave his patronage to a Yorkshire meeting and drafted its resolutions of 14 October. These demanded a meeting of Parliament to inquire into the events at Manchester, affirmed the right of public assembly and expressed sympathy with the distressed lower orders. Fitzwilliam took especial exception to 'the approbation given in the name of the crown to the use, in the first instance, of a military body in the execution of a civil process', claiming that this smacked of continental practices whereby the military power of the crown rode roughshod (in this instance literally) over the constitutionally enshrined rights of the common people.

It was ironic, and indicative of the triumph of perceived party political advantage over principle, that Fitzwilliam had himself forcibly dispersed a gathering at Sheffield in 1795 at the head of a yeomanry troop, and had not felt moved to condemn a charge of Hussars against food rioters at Sheffield in 1812.

The government responded swiftly to the challenge when, on 21 October, Sidmouth gave Fitzwilliam notice to quit his lord-lieutenancy. His action not only added to the impression that the government was engaged in arbitrary and high-handed actions; it provided constitutional Whiggism with a martyr around whom to rally (albeit one who had lost office rather than life) and facilitated the Whigs' displacement of the radicals at the head of the popular clamour for reform.

Fitzwilliam's elevation to heroic status was a mixed blessing for the Whig leadership, however. On the one hand, he had long been a central figure in the connections that made up the Whig party; a nephew of Rockingham and the closest friend of Charles James Fox, he was a leading exponent of the views of Edmund Burke and was first uncle by marriage and later father-in-law of Earl Grey himself. Born in 1748, he played an important part in transmitting the eighteenth-century traditions of the Whigs into the nineteenth century. On the other hand, he was known as a staunch opponent of parliamentary reform; as Grey confessed, 'there is nothing so hopeless as the idea of gaining his acquiescence in *any* measure of parliamentary reform'.

Fitzwilliam's attitude thus made his criticism of Peterloo all the more damning but also constrained Grey, for the forseeable future, from an even more radical outflanking of the radicals by committing the Whigs to a programme of parliamentary reform. By his action and beliefs Fitzwilliam was thus instrumental both in taking the initiative from the radicals and in ensuring that criticism was channelled into denunciations of personalities rather than a critique of the parliamentary system.

The speedy approval given to the Manchester authorities by the government led to the equally speedy disapproval of that approbation by the Whigs, which in turn precipitated the dismissal of Fitzwilliam, the recall of Parliament in November 1819 and the government's decision to hobble further Whig or radical mischief-making by means of six new pieces of legislation.

The so-called Six Acts of 1819 consisted of the Seditious Meetings Act, the Training Prevention Act, the Seizure of Arms Act, the Misdemeanours Act, the Blasphemous and Seditious Libels Act and the Newspaper Stamp Duties Act. Like Peterloo they have entered into the popular folk memory as epitomising a repressive and reactionary regime. However, in this respect, as in so many others, the popular folk memory is seriously defective.

The Seditious Meetings Act restricted public meetings considering 'any public Grievance or any Matter on Church and State' (except those called by 'known constituted authorities') to parish level, and obliged the organisers to give the local magistrates notice of the time and place of such meetings, which they might then alter at their own discretion so as to preempt any attempt at mass insurrection through simultaneous meetings. Thus this Act, like its namesake of 1817–8, was an attempt to prevent any abuse of the right of assembly like that which had occurred at Spa Fields in December 1816.

The Training Prevention Act prohibited paramilitary training whilst the Seizure of Arms Act permitted the seizure of arms 'dangerous to the Public Peace'. Even today such measures would be regarded by most people as conducive to the public good.

The Misdemeanours Act made it more difficult for the accused to exploit delays in the judicial process and to get themselves released on bail. Even if this was considered objectionable, it was certainly preferable to the further suspension of Habeas Corpus.

31

The Blasphemous and Seditious Libels Act strengthened previous legislation of this nature by laying down banishment or transportation for fourteen years as the maximum penalty for a second conviction, and giving magistrates the right to search for and confiscate all copies of libellous materials in the possession of the offender.

The Newspaper Stamp Duties Act was directed against 'pamphlets and printed materials containing observations on public events and occurrences tending to excite hatred and contempt of the Government and Constitution of these realms as by law established, and also vilifying our holy religion'. Publishers and printers of material containing 'Public News, Intelligence or Occurrences, or any Remarks or Observation thereon' were ordered to provide sureties of their good behaviour by entering into recognizances as a guarantee of payment if found guilty of libel. Moreover, if newspapers appeared at least once every twenty-six days, and retailed for sixpence or less, then they became liable to the stamp duty of fourpence which Vansittart had levied in 1815. Thus the effect of the Act was to restrict the freedom of the press insofar as it effectively restricted the circulation of newspapers by obliging them to raise their prices to cover the costs of the stamp duty. It also increased the penalties for any lapse of self-censorship which resulted in successful prosecutions for libel.

When one takes into account the facts that the Newspaper Stamp Duties, Blasphemous and Seditious Libels, and Misdemeanours Acts were chiefly concerned to plug loopholes in existing laws, that the Training Prevention Act would hardly offend even the most anxious of contemporary civil rights activists, and that the Seizure of Arms and Seditious Meetings Acts were temporary and were not renewed or replaced, it is difficult not to agree with Gash's contention that 'The sinister reputation of the Six Acts ... is hardly borne out by an examination of their contents' and that they should be criticised not on the grounds 'that they were a powerful instrument in the hands of the executive' but because 'for the most part they were misdirected and ineffective', as shown, most graphically, by the disorder which centred around Queen Caroline in the years 1820–21.

In the short term, however, repressive measures seemed to be vindicated when on 23 February 1820 a group of Spencean

veterans of Spa Fields, led by Arthur Thistlewood, were appre-
hended by twelve Bow Street runners and a detachment of the
Coldstream Guards in a loft over a range of coach-houses in
Cato Street, off the Edgware Road. Their offence was to have
plotted to assassinate the entire British Cabinet as it dined at the
Earl of Harrowby's in Grosvenor Square.

Thistlewood and four of his fellow Cato Street conspirators
were found guilty of high treason, and were hanged until dead
and then decapitated on 1 May 1820. The other conspirators
were transported, along with six men who in March 1820 had
been part of an assembly of roughly three hundred men who had
met near Huddersfield to express their sympathy with the
conspirators.

In fact, the Cato Street conspirators had never seriously
threatened the lives of anyone but themselves as George
Edwards, the secretary of a Spencean section, had kept the
authorities informed throughout, and may well have acted as an
agent provocateur.

But if Thistlewood failed to destroy the cabinet, Queen
Caroline almost succeeded in bringing down the entire government shortly afterwards.

The future Prince Regent had married his first cousin in 1794
but the couple had separated by 1796 and Caroline had returned
to the continent in 1814. George repeatedly requested his
ministers to arrange a divorce on the grounds of Caroline's
alleged adultery, but Liverpool was reluctant to follow this path
as neither the evidence of Caroline's adultery nor George's own
behaviour was beyond reproach.

Whether Caroline was more sinned against than sinning was
a delicate calculation but there is no doubt that the British
public preferred to look upon her as the wronged party as a
means of legitimately expressing its intense loathing of her
husband. When George III died in January 1820 Caroline could
not be dissuaded from returning to Britain to claim her rights
as queen and Liverpool could no longer dissuade George from
trying to obtain a divorce. However, the government was caught
between the King on the one hand and pro-Caroline public
opinion on the other as the royal divorce was to be accom-
plished by a Bill of Pains and Penalties which would also deprive
Caroline of the title and rights of queen.

For nine days after Caroline's triumphal return to London on

6 June 1820 the capital experienced serious rioting, in the course of which the Home Secretary himself led a troop of the Life Guards in defending his property. Most ominously it appeared that on this occasion the loyalty of all the King's men might not be taken for granted: soldiers of the Household Brigade were rumoured to drink the Queen's health; those soldiers posted outside the King's residence at Carlton House saluted the Queen as her procession passed; and on 15 June there was a mutiny in the 3rd regiment of Foot Guards which resulted in the despatch of the regiment to Portsmouth on the following day.

On 10 November the government's majority in the Lords dropped to nine on the third reading of the Bill. This meant that the Bill's defeat in the Commons was almost certain, given the government's smaller majority, weaker debating team and greater responsiveness to extra-parliamentary pressures there. Liverpool thus triggered more riotous celebration amongst Caroline's supporters and angered the King by publicly abandoning the Bill.

The government nevertheless maintained that Caroline's adultery had been proved and she was refused admittance to Westminster Abbey when George was crowned in July 1821 and the door of Westminster Hall was slammed in her face when she attempted to gatecrash the Coronation banquet.

She was taken ill on the following day and died of peritonitis on 7 August 1821, having had no time to enjoy the financial settlement which she had finally been prevailed upon to accept, and before her former supporters' disillusionment with her over this pay-off had had time to take root.

Caroline chose 'The injured Queen of England' as the inscription on her coffin, and her desire to be buried beside her father in Brunswick provided the opportunity for her supporters to stage one final riot on her behalf, as an unseemly struggle broke out over the route of her funeral procession as it made its way through London to Harwich. The government routed the cortège so as to avoid the City of London, a notorious centre of pro-Caroline sentiment. The Common Council of the City of London nevertheless unanimously voted on 13 August to meet the funeral procession and conduct it through the city. At Cumberland Gate (on the site of the present-day Marble Arch) seventy-five of the Life Guards responded to stoning by the pro-Caroline crowd – during which thirty-seven of their number and eight of their horses were wounded – by opening fire, killing two of the rioters and wounding many others.

However, the rioters succeeded in their objective of forcing the funeral procession to be re-routed through the City of London. Civil Under-Secretary Henry Hobhouse expressed the government's dread that the mob would be seen to have 'carried their object by force, and . . . beaten the Military' and Sidmouth himself wrote of 'a Crisis, at which the Authority and Reputation of the Government will be strengthened and raised, or irrevocably lost'.

The search for scapegoats by the authorities led to the dismissal in September of Sir Robert Baker as the senior magistrate at Bow Street, and of Major-General Sir Robert Wilson from the army. The former had headed the procession and had apparently lost his nerve in allowing the cortège to be diverted from its original route, whilst the latter had intervened to reprimand Captain Oakes and his men for firing upon the crowd at Cumberland Gate.

Four months after 'Carol-loo', as this incident was unimaginatively named, Sidmouth, who had already indicated a willingness to vacate his position, resigned as Home Secretary, to be succeeded by Robert Peel. However, the political repercussions of the Queen Caroline affair were much greater than the embarrassment of Sidmouth (who remained in the cabinet as Minister without Portfolio)

The affair weakened the government in three important respects and brought it closer to destruction than at any time before or after. First, the affair monopolised the time and energies of the government, so that potentially popular reforms such as the abolition or reduction of tariffs were delayed.

Second, the affair occasioned Canning's resignation from the government in mid-December 1820, once again enfeebling its front bench in the Commons. Canning maintained that notwithstanding the evidence of Caroline's alleged adultery, the queen was innocent until proven guilty and he had only agreed to the omission of her name from the liturgy (which could be regarded as prejudging the case) on the grounds that this omission would inevitably form part of any negotiated settlement. In theory he resigned because Liverpool's government refused to treat Caroline as if the abandonment of the Bill were tantamount to her exoneration. In practice, however, Canning's action looked like that of a rat leaving what appeared to be a sinking ship. Although the ministry did in fact stay afloat the lack of ballast on the Commons front bench was not immediately rectified, as Peel, who had resigned as Irish Chief Secretary in 1818, had refused to return to the government in Canning's place (holding out until he was offered the Home Office) and Bragge-Bathurst thus temporarily assumed responsibility for the Board of Control.

Third, the affair irrevocably soured the king's already strained relations with Liverpool. George felt that Liverpool had mishandled the affair throughout, and Canning's expression of his 'unabated esteem and respect for the Queen' in the Commons whilst still a member of the government rubbed salt into the wounds.

Moreover, the king cannot have been pleased that only three members of the cabinet, Liverpool, Eldon and Harrowby, spoke on behalf of the Bill of Pains and Penalties, and would certainly have disapproved of the fact that no ministerial pressure was brought to bear on peers friendly to the government, despite the fact that the Whigs treated the affair as a party issue. Given his history of opposition to any suggestion of royal divorce it seems reasonable to assume that Liverpool's heart was simply not in the matter, not because of his respect for the sanctity of holy matrimony but rather because he was under no illusions regarding the political difficulties of securing a divorce. The 'Carolloo' incident further undermined George's confidence in his prime minister as the government had disregarded his sensible instructions that Caroline's remains should be transported to Harwich by water rather than by land. Henceforth it was Castlereagh, Sidmouth, Wellington and Canning (who returned to office in 1822 and had ingratiated himself with the king by the spring of 1825) rather than Liverpool who had to smooth the government's relations with the monarch.

Having considered those factors which combined to produce popular unrest and examined the main instances of disorder in the period 1812–21, it is now appropriate to consider the question whether that unrest was, in fact, severely repressed.

It should of course be pointed out that it is possible to argue that the reaction of the authorities – or at least of the central authorities – to popular unrest was not particularly severe, despite the fact that the wild rhetoric and actions of some radicals (notably the Spenceans) combined with genuine and widespread hardship to make the prospect of degeneration into a French-style revolution seem credible at times. In the authorities' defence it is also worth remembering how pitifully small were the forces at their disposal for maintaining law and order, given the absence of anything resembling a modern police force. Hence the government's recourse to spies and informers.

The use of *agents provocateurs* was, however, particularly damaging to the government's reputation in the eyes of contemporaries and posterity alike, insofar as it 'exposed the Government to the charge of fabricating plots in order to suppress them, of resorting to continental methods of repression, and of generally running away from its own shadow', in White's words.

Gash concedes that the use of such agents was 'a hazardous practice' as they tended to view economic disputes as politically motivated and to exaggerate the size and importance of the organisations which they revealed, and as they may even have succeeded in egging on individuals to commit illegal acts which they might otherwise have refrained from committing. Thus 'at best they were defective and at worst deceptive instruments'; the authorities' reliance upon them indicates the extent of their desperation, given the poverty of alternative means of law enforcement.

Given the above, the essential moderation of the government's response is all the more surprising and commendable for, as has already been pointed out, the partial suspension of Habeas Corpus and the Seditious Meetings Act of 1817 were both allowed to lapse in 1818; Peterloo occurred despite, rather than because of, Home Office advice; and the Six Acts which followed did not, on the whole, either in intention or in execution, pose a significant threat to civil liberties.

Even more surprising perhaps is the fact that as regards purely industrial disputes, Sidmouth's Home Office took the course of conciliation rather than repression, for although the Combination Laws remained on the statute book throughout this period, requests to strengthen them were denied, and during the Tyneside disturbances of 1815 and the Manchester weavers' strike of 1818, the Home Office was critical of the employers and sympathetic towards their respective labour forces.

To sum up, men like Liverpool and Castlereagh (who had both incidentally experienced revolutionary France at first hand) were faced with problems that were unprecedented in their number, complexity and scope. Moreover, they had to deal with these problems, and particularly those relating to law enforcement, with few – if any – and often defective tools at their disposal. When all these facts are taken into account it can be seen that studied restraint and considered moderation rather than needless severity and reckless repression characterised the response of Liverpool's government to public unrest in the period 1812–21.

Moreover, when conditions allowed – once the economy had improved and the Queen Caroline affair had ceased to act as a distraction – Liverpool's government embarked upon reform or, to be more precise, continued along the path of economic reform upon which it had already embarked, with increasing vigour.

5

The government's record on reform

The Queen Caroline affair which erupted in 1820 came close to wrecking Liverpool's government as he attempted to steer a middle course between pro-Caroline public opinion and the king. However, in the course of the next three years the remodelled ministry – which now had both Peel and Canning back on board – regained its stability, gained a new lease of life and began to embark upon a course in foreign and domestic affairs which some have regarded as a liberal departure from previous practice.

Indeed, in *Lord Liverpool and Liberal Toryism*, published in 1941, W.R. Brock coined the term 'Liberal Toryism' to describe this phenomenon, and since that time it has often been claimed that the period of Tory rule from 1812 to 1827 (or even to 1830) should be divided into 'repressive' and 'liberal' phases around the year 1822.

Following Brock, it became orthodox to take the view that from 1812 to 1821–3 the Liverpool government was reactionary and repressive as shown, for example, by its support for the Holy Alliance powers abroad and for the magistrates responsible for Peterloo at home, and by acts such as the introduction of the Corn Law in 1815 and repeal of the income tax in 1816. However, a change of personnel between 1821–3 allegedly resulted in a significant shift in the nature of the government.

Three changes are regarded as possessing particular significance: the replacement of Castlereagh by Canning as Foreign Secretary and Leader of the House of Commons; the replacement of Sidmouth by Peel as Home Secretary; and the replacement of Vansittart by Robinson as Chancellor of the Exchequer. The first three were identified with cooperation with the Holy Alliance abroad and the maintenance of draconian penalties for criminals and high tariffs at home, whereas the last three were identified with championing liberalism both abroad and at home, including the relaxation of the criminal code and the freeing of trade.

The period 1822–7 certainly witnessed a series of important reforms. These included the 1823 Reciprocity of Duties Act, which modified the seventeenth-century Navigation Laws and ushered in a new commercial relationship between Britain and her colonies; the 1823 and 1824 Gaols Acts, which ensured that every county or riding and town maintained a gaol or house of correction, which was subject to Home Office scrutiny; the 1824 repeal of the Combination Laws, which legalised trade unions; the 1825 Juries Regulation Act, which clarified the law regarding jury selection and responsibilities; the 1826 Bank Act, which restricted note issue and encouraged the formation of joint-stock banks; and the legal reforms of 1825–8, which repealed 278 Acts and summarised those of their provisions which were retained within eight Acts.

If one considers the period of Tory rule up to 1830 one could add the 1828 modification of the Corn Laws and Repeal of the Test and Corporation Acts, the 1829 Metropolitan Police Act and Catholic Emancipation Act, and the 1830 Act for the Consolidation of the Forgery Laws.

Moreover, Britain's 'liberal' foreign policy over this same period witnessed recognition of the independent republics of Buenos Aires, Mexico and Colombia in 1824, and of Brazil in 1825, the despatching of forces to assist the cause of liberalism in Portugal in 1826, and joint action with France and Russia in 1827 to secure Greek independence from the Turks.

It might nevertheless be objected that the term 'Liberal Toryism', when used to describe such policies or the perspective which supposedly informed them, is anachronistic. In fact, Brock quite openly admits that 'The name is artificial – that is to say it is not found in the mouths of contemporaries.' Brock nevertheless considers the term to be of value 'because the High

Tories accused the Government of "liberalism" . . . because the "liberals" who dominated the Cabinet felt acutely their estrangement from the "ultras", and because the meaning of the phrase is readily intelligible to a later age'.

However, each of these points is open to question. Some contemporaries, including Peel, were certainly apt to regard 'more liberal' as 'an odious but intelligible phrase' and might thus condemn specific government policies as being 'liberal'. Whether it follows from this that the phrase 'Liberal Toryism' can be meaningfully applied remains, however, problematical.

At the heart of this difficulty is the fact that Brock's use of the abstract noun 'Liberal Toryism' implies a political philosophy or system of thought which is peculiarly unsuited to the pragmatism of politicians such as Canning. As Brock himself remarks, Canning's opponents called him a liberal, not because of 'his approval of popular revolts, for even they knew how guarded that approval was' but rather 'because he brought in public opinion as his ally' by 'his oratory, and his publication, when it suited him, of diplomatic correspondence which a more timid – or, his opponents would add, a more gentlemanly – minister would have regarded as secret'.

Thus Brock presents Canning as being perceived as 'liberal' not because his foreign policy objectives were actually liberal or were seen as liberal but rather because his means of conducting foreign policy were often condemned by contemporaries as being liberal.

Brock also contradicts himself in claiming that 'the "liberals" . . . dominated the Cabinet', as he later writes that in 1823 'The High Tories could command six [Wellington, Eldon, Sidmouth, Bathurst, Westmorland and Melville], the 'liberals' three [Canning, Robinson and Huskisson] with a probable three more [Harrowby, Wynn and Bexley], so that the votes of Peel and Liverpool were crucial.' However, given that Liverpool always sided with Canning, his authority 'provided a united Cabinet in place of deadlock'. Admittedly Brock later states that when 'Sidmouth . . . resigned after the Cabinet of 6 December [1824] . . . the "Ultras" were in a minority', but it is difficult even then to speak of the 'liberals', as dominating the cabinet if one accepts his detailed analysis of the balance of forces within it. Nor can it be claimed that the so-called 'liberals' dominated the 'inner cabinet', as Brock quotes Wynn as expressing the belief

41

'that the only real and efficient cabinet upon all matters consists of Lords Liverpool and Bathurst, the Duke of Wellington and Canning'.

There are other arguments which suggest that Brock has overdramatised the impact of the ministerial changes of 1821–3 by dividing the period into distinctively 'repressive' and 'liberal' Tory phases. In the first place, it is worth making the obvious point that Liverpool actively presided over the entire period of 1812–27 and thereby imparted a fundamental continuity in terms of outlook and policy.

Second, the 'new' men of 1821–3 were not really new because they had all served under Liverpool prior to 1822. As has been mentioned above, although Canning passed up the opportunity of becoming Foreign Secretary in 1812 because he also insisted on the Leadership of the House of Commons, he did enter the government as President of the Board of Control in 1816, only to resign the post over the Queen Caroline affair in December 1820.

Robinson – who was regarded as a follower and client of the supposedly reactionary Castlereagh – had been Vice-President (1812–18) and then President of the Board of Trade (1818–23) before becoming Chancellor of the Exchequer. Moreover, according to Boyd Hilton 'Robinson was selected, not for any professional attributes, but as a sop to "Van"' – as Vansittart would have felt disgraced if replaced by Huskisson – 'and to the squires' who regarded his parliamentary manners as pleasing. As Bathurst remarked to Harrowby, 'Robinson's succession to the office . . . keeps more in the background *one* of the real objects of the Change, viz. Huskisson's promotion' to the Presidency of the Board of Trade.

Huskisson had been First Commissioner of Woods and Forests since 1814, from which time he had been, according to Brock, the Prime Minister's 'intimate economic adviser' alongside Vansittart, Robinson and Long, and in Boyd Hilton's expert opinion had become the key member of this informal economic committee by 1819.

Peel had been Chief Secretary for Ireland between 1812 and 1818 and had chaired the Currency Commission which had recommended a phased return to the gold standard in its report of 1819.

In short, although the ministerial reshuffle of 1821–3 did

bring new men to the top, their rise can hardly be described as meteoric and they cannot be absolved of involvement in the supposedly reactionary policies of the Liverpool government's prior to 1822.

Nor was it the case that the 'old' men associated with the policies of reaction all disappeared from the political stage as abruptly as Londonderry (as Castlereagh had become when he succeeded his father as the second marquess in April 1821). He slit his throat with a penknife on 12 August 1822, in a state of depression induced by overwork and by his being blackmailed (or in the paranoid belief that he was being blackmailed) for illegally engaging in homosexual practices.

Vansittart, as Lord Bexley (whom Brock depicts as likely to side with the 'liberals' in Cabinet although Gash characterises him as a 'Protestant' Tory), became Chancellor of the Duchy of Lancaster, whilst Sidmouth was a member of the cabinet without portfolio until his resignation in December 1824, and Eldon and Wellington remained as Lord Chancellor and Master-General of Ordnance respectively to the very end of Liverpool's ministry in 1827.

As has already been suggested, it can be argued that the period prior to 1822 is not as black a period of reaction as it has commonly been painted, in that the repressive measures of the period represent a studiously moderate reaction to specific disturbances and the government took, or attempted to take, a series of measures which belie its image as hostile to the interests of the working class.

In support of the latter contention it is worth remembering Boyd Hilton's remark that whereas the landed interest regarded the 1815 Corn Law 'as a permanent (or at least long-term) endeavour to maintain prices; ministers related it specifically to the transition that had to be made from war to peace, and from a depreciated paper currency to a metallic standard'. Moreover, the 1815 Corn Law was designed to protect that sector of the economy which employed by far the largest number of people, and the prosperity of which was considered, in line with physiocratic thought, to be the bedrock of the economy as a whole. It is also important to remember that Liverpool and Vansittart had wanted to retain the income tax in 1816 and that it was only because repeal was forced upon them by the backbenches that they were ultimately obliged to resort to additional indirect taxes (which hit the poor disproportionately hard) and delay the freeing of trade.

The government's concern for the welfare of the working class is even more clearly illustrated by those occasions (such as on Tyneside in 1815 and in Manchester in 1818) on which the government expressed criticism of employers and sympathy towards their workforces when the two sides were in dispute.

Although the flow of blood may have been staunched after 1821 it would a mistake to view the period thereafter as free from bloodletting. For example, five civilians were killed in Sunderland in 1825 in a clash between a troop of dragoons and those attempting to prevent ships from sailing with non-union crews, and in 1826 six civilians were killed in a clash with troops at a mill in Bolton.

More fundamentally, the notion that the period of Tory rule can be neatly divided into reactionary and reformist phases can be challenged on the grounds that not all legislation prior to 1822 was repressive, even allowing for the fact that one person's reform – such as the 1814 Peace Preservation Act, creating a special police force for Ireland – can be another person's repression. Even the 1815 Corn Law had a free trade dimension in so far as foreign corn was to continue to be warehoused duty-free (free bonding) and was supplemented by the Assize of Bread Repeal Act which opened up to competition the manufacturing and retailing of bread.

1812 saw two Relief Acts for Dissenters, and the Unitarians were brought within the terms of earlier legislation by means of the 1813 Toleration Act. Absenteeism in the Church was legislated against in both 1813 and 1817. In 1813 those clauses in the Elizabethan Statute of Artificers which empowered judges to fix wages were repealed and in 1814 the statute's regulations regarding apprenticeship were also repealed.

Proposed and actual reforms indisputably increased in number following the final defeat of France in 1815. Thus 1816 witnessed a restriction in the use of the pillory, the revenues of Great Britain and Ireland were united in a single Consolidated Fund under the direction of the United Kingdom Treasury, and the first step towards a unified civil service was taken when the salaries of officials in public offices were made subject to parliamentary approval.

In 1817, in addition to the sweeping away of a mass of

political sinecures, there was an Act to protect and encourage savings, a Passenger Transport Act to facilitate emigration, and a Truck Act to curb the system whereby wages were sometimes paid or partly paid in vouchers which could only be exchanged for over-priced goods at shops run by the employer. The Poor Employment Act was also passed, and this made available state loans totalling £500,000 for the mainland and £250,000 for Ireland for encouraging the fisheries and public works undertaken by local authorities.

In 1818 the government not only passed an act whereby a Church Building Commission was placed in charge of a grant of £1,000,000 towards the building of new Anglican churches (to be followed by an additional £500,000 in 1824) but also provided for the easier creation of new parishes, thus going some way towards meeting the spiritual needs of the new towns.

The 1819 decision to return to the gold standard by 1823, although deflationary in the short term, was a retrospective act of justice to creditors which helped to underpin future prosperity by stabilising the currency, whilst the Bank Advances Act of the same year further defined the relations between the Treasury and the Bank of England by subjecting the latter's future advances to the government to parliamentary scrutiny.

The 1819 Factory Act, brought forward by the elder Robert Peel and supported by Liverpool, banned the employment of children under nine in cotton mills and factories and limited the working hours of young persons under sixteen to twelve per day exclusive of the time allowed for meals. A Commons Committee of Inquiry was also set up with government support in 1819 to study the weaknesses of the legal system.

1820 saw the abolition of the whipping of women and witnessed reforms in the Treasury, including the First Lord's dispensing with his powers of patronage in the Customs, which represent a landmark in the development of the civil service as a non-political career open to the talents: a classical liberal aim.

It was, however, in the fields of finance and free trade that the government prior to 1822 most clearly engaged in the spadework which bore fruit in the period after 1822.

Robinson was able to inherit a sound financial system because Liverpool and Vansittart had already, in 1819, embarked upon a new financial policy, involving taking £12 million from the Sinking Fund (a policy which had been rejected on political grounds in the immediate aftermath of the repeal of income tax) and raising £3 million in new taxes, including a new malt tax, which placed the budget in surplus and the government in political credit. Robinson thus reaped the rewards of Vansittart's hard work and returning prosperity.

Brock also concedes that 'the beginnings of free trade legislation in England can be definitely dated in 1820' if one considers Liverpool's speech in favour of free trade of 26 May 1820 and the pioneering work of Robinson's successor as Vice-President of the Board of Trade, Thomas Wallace. It was Wallace who promoted the entrepôt or transit trade by recommending the relaxation of the Navigation Laws, the reduction of pilot, light, and harbour dues, and an extension of free bonding in British warehouses so as to include even those manufactures whose importation for consumption was forbidden.

Liverpool characteristically proceeded cautiously for fear of alienating vested interests. Nevertheless, he argued in 1820 that Britain had risen to greatness not because of, but in spite of, its protectionist system, and clearly expressed his intention to relax that system. This liberalisation of the economy worked, for despite reductions in the duties on rum, coal, wool and silk in his 1824 budget Robinson enjoyed a surplus nearly three times as great as the anticipated £500,000 by the time of his 1825 budget, and was thus able to free trade still further by large reductions in the duties on spirits, wine, rum, cider, coffee and hemp. However, it was Wallace who had taken what he himself described as 'the first step in receding from a system detrimental to our commercial relations', and which Barry Gordon describes as 'the first practical step towards implementation of *laissez-faire* in the post-war period', in reducing the difference in duty paid on Baltic as against Canadian timber in 1821, although Boyd Hilton rightly stresses that its significance was chiefly symbolic as 'it was too slight a reform to affect the disposition of the timber trade very seriously' and that the move was characteristically 'conceived in terms of regulating and restraining rather than extending commerce'.

Gash is therefore right, on balance, to express the view that '"Prosperity" Robinson earned both his nickname and a credit for his finance which more justly belonged to the administration as a whole, including those forgotten men Vansittart and Wallace.'

Boyd Hilton's analysis differs from Gordon's in as much as he claims that it is anachronistic to regard the reluctance of Liverpool's government to interfere with the economy 'as evidence of a *laissez-faire* commitment, and a pointer towards the age of free trade'. He claims that this reluctance signified the operation of short-term considerations rather than the application of a far-sighted economic ideology as 'the commercial reforms of the 1820s . . . were geared', like the return to the gold standard in 1819, 'less to expanding Britain's exports artificially than to attracting foreign goods and capital into British warehouses and funds'. In short, free trade commercial reforms were predicated upon monetary, revenue and agricultural policies and were initiated 'to restrict indiscriminate growth and to stabilize rather than to expand the economy'.

However, the key point in the current context is that Boyd Hilton also denies the claim that 1822 should be regarded as a watershed. Thus, he writes that 'the important break in official thought on agricultural protection between 1815 and 1846' occurred with the Agricultural Report of 1821, as the Irish potato blight of 1816-7 knocked a hole in the belief that the United Kingdom could feed itself, and the Corn Law came increasingly to be regarded as an obstacle to Britain's obtaining the importation of necessary foodstuffs from the continent. Thus 'the move away from protection . . . was not the consequence of an ideological conversion to free trade, nor of a political appeal to new industrial or commercial classes, but . . . an adjustment to altered conditions of supply'.

Ricardianism and theories of international comparative advantage were adopted by the Liverpool government after 1821 to justify and rationalise a change of policy which was driven by *pragmatic* considerations so that, in Boyd Hilton's words, the 'changeover to an export philosophy was not the cause of the *volte-face* on corn law policy, but a result of it'.

Free trade was only erected into a dogmatic 'system' when the government's economic policy was subjected to intense criticism in the light of the onset of commercial and manufacturing depression in 1826, and even then it was pursued as the best means of preparing Britain for hostilities (by facilitating the creation of private wealth that could be tapped in an emergency) not, as was later the case with the Manchester School, as the means of spreading international prosperity and peace.

47

In terms of foreign policy, too, the contrast between the periods before and after 1822 has been overdrawn. The simplistic traditional view contemporary with Brock was that Castlereagh was a reactionary who colluded with the European autocrats in their bid to crush liberalism and nationalism, whilst Canning was a liberal who championed liberal and nationalist movements on the continent and in the New World. In fact, it has long been recognised that Castlereagh was not so reactionary and that Canning was not so liberal as used to be supposed.

Whilst the two men possessed conflicting personalities and were bitter personal rivals who cordially detested one another, the policies which they pursued at the Foreign Office differed in terms of presentation rather than substance. Castlereagh, the reserved loner, was a poor public speaker who only impressed by virtue of mastery of his briefs and by transparent sincerity. Canning was eloquent and flamboyant, self-confident and self-promotional. The former was as incapable of 'playing to the gallery' as the latter was incapable of resisting this temptation. As Brougham put it in 1822: 'Canning succeeds to Foreign Office, lead of House, &c. – in short, all of Castlereagh except his good judgement, good manners and bad English.'

It is true that Castlereagh welcomed the prospect of regular Congresses or summit meetings between the Great Powers, under the terms of Article VI of the Quadruple Alliance of 1815, but he was notoriously critical of the Holy Alliance, which he famously regarded as a 'piece of sublime mysticism and non-sense' and which he prevented the Prince Regent from joining, proposing instead that the prince should avoid giving un-necessary offence to the Czar, whose brainchild it was, by signing merely as an expression of his private approval of the Alliance's aims.

Moreover, when the Holy Alliance powers of Russia, Austria, and Prussia hijacked the 1820 Congress of Troppau for their own anti-liberal and anti-nationalist ends, Castlereagh only sent an observer, and he formally broke with his former allies when, in his State Paper of May 1820, he denounced their assertion in the Troppau Protocol of a general right to suppress revolution.

Even Brock admits that 'Castlereagh was already moving slowly, perhaps reluctantly, along the road which Canning was to follow with spirit and enthusiasm', and Canning himself admitted that on becoming Foreign Secretary in 1822 'I found in the records of my office a state paper, laying down the principle of non-interference with all the qualification properly belonging to it'. Typically, Canning could not bear to praise Castlereagh by name even posthumously but the important point is that he himself clearly accepted that the latter's State Paper of May 1820 provided the correct basis for the policy which Britain should pursue in response to the Troppau Protocol.

Similarly, Gash points out that Canning's policy of recognising the rebellious Spanish colonies was not new but was 'merely a continuation and enlargement of one started by Castlereagh', who had already conceded belligerent status to the South American rebels. Intervention in Portugal in 1826 in response to an appeal from the regency government, which occasioned Canning's famous words about calling the New World into existence to redress the balance of the Old, was actually unavoidable under the terms of treaty obligations and self-interest rather than a disinterested liberal policy initiative.

And if Castlereagh laid the foundations for Canning's foreign policy, the same can be said for several of Castlereagh's colleagues in relation to their successors, again undermining the notion that the years 1821–3 signify a major discontinuity in the nature of the ministry. Thus Sidmouth prepared a first draft of some of Peel's reforms of the criminal code and, as has been shown above, Robinson as Chancellor of the Exchequer greatly profited from the work of Liverpool and Vansittart, whilst Huskisson greatly benefited from the pioneering work done by Wallace.

Nor, according to Brock, can Huskisson receive the full credit for the 1823 Trade Duties Reciprocity Act (which empowered the King in Council to allow the ships of any nation to transport goods to the United Kingdom on the same terms as British ships were allowed entry to their ports), as much of the actual work was done by 'a hard working civil servant, J[ames]. D. Hume', secretary of the Customs, under Huskisson's supervision.

Furthermore, the 1824 repeal of the Combination Laws 'was not the work of the ministers', says Brock; 'indeed it passed without their serious consideration', as the result of the efforts of the radicals Place, Burdett and Joseph Hume. And when repeal was followed by a wave of labour disputes, Wallace was appointed the chairman of a committee which recommended an illiberal Amending Act, the upshot of which was that all combinations except those to fix hours and wages were made illegal and magistrates were given summary powers to punish any man using force to compel membership of an association or participation in a strike.

The liberal credentials of Liverpool's ministry after 1822 can also be called into question on the grounds that there was still no prospect of Catholic emancipation or parliamentary reform, as many Tories opposed the former and all were opposed to the latter.

Moreover, there is good reason to dispute the application of the 'Liberal Tory' label to Peel. He once characterised the phrase 'more liberal' as 'intelligible' but 'odious' and even more revealing is his comment in his 1827 resignation speech that he might justly be characterised as 'an illiberal'.

In the light of the above, it may be worth asking whether Peel's abolition of the death penalty for numerous offences was motivated not by liberal–humanitarian considerations but rather by a simple desire to secure a greater number of convictions given that it was widely felt that juries sometimes acquitted the blatantly guilty under the old system, because they felt that their crime did not merit hanging.

In an important review article D.E.D. Beales has argued that the tendency of Peel's apologists to exaggerate his commitment to reform in his early career is most marked with regard to these very legal reforms and has pointed out that compared with Russell, Home Secretary between 1835 and 1839, Peel merely 'tinkered', as the 'mitigations of the law's severity with which he is so generally credited . . . amounted only to repealing statutes and sections of statutes which were totally disused, and to a more generous commutation policy'. Gattrell has even gone so far as to state that 'Peel's interest in criminal law reform had less to do with repudiating the barbarism of past times than . . . restoring the law's credibility against public attack, and . . . in making it . . . even more punitive – more of a terror, not less'.

Peel's record on prison reform is also not quite as impressive as appears at first sight. Although Gash is favourably disposed towards Peel, he points out that the 1823 Gaols Act had been prepared by a parliamentary committee and accepted by the government in 1821, so that 'In placing it on the statute book

Peel had acted more as a midwife than as a parent'. Brock certainly does not make the mistake of many of his successors in labelling Peel as a Liberal Tory.

But then we are left with a 'gang of three', comprising Canning, Huskisson and Robinson, all of whose policies on closer inspection become barely, if at all, distinguishable in substance from those of their predecessors. Indeed, when subjected to detailed scrutiny, Liberal Toryism virtually disappears as a coherent set of values or policies, as does the division between the 'repressive' and 'liberal' phases of Tory rule.

This is not, of course, to deny that the government and governing of Britain changed around the year 1822. Any ministerial reshuffle involving such key posts as those of the Home Secretary, Foreign Secretary and Chancellor of the Exchequer is likely to have an impact. The pace of reform certainly picked up as the period progressed – at least in economic affairs – but this was not due, as Boyd Hilton reminds us, to 'any significant liberalization of policy or radical substitution of the men most responsible for economic decisions' but was rather 'rendered possible by the possession of a revenue surplus and by improvements in the government's political situation'.

Moreover, not all reforms, as the 1824 Repeal of the Combination Laws reminds us, can be credited to the government, whilst the watershed in this regard predated the change in officeholders and related rather to the end of the wars with France and the gradual cessation of public disorder as the problems attending the transition from war to peacetime ended, and the economy gradually picked up. The Queen Caroline affair has muddied the waters, since the disorders which it generated have helped to obscure the reforms of the period prior to 1822 and bolstered the impression that disorder was endemic in the decade between 1811 and 1821.

Thus, when the years immediately preceding and succeeding 1822 are considered, the similarities outweigh the differences and the differences were, in any case, differences in personnel rather than policy, presentation rather than principle, and style rather than substance. The government was better able to present its case in the Commons than hitherto, but the principles underlying its arguments had not undergone a radical revision. This is not to deny the importance of presentation and style in politics, but it is salutary to remember that these factors mattered much less in the age of Lord Liverpool than they do now, in the age of the spindoctor, the electronic mass media and a mass electorate.

6

Liverpool's record as premier

Near the end of his political career, Liverpool wrote that 'The world will at least give me credit for my ecclesiastical promotions, whatever they may say or think of me in other respects'. Gash makes a possible exception of Liverpool's appointment of his cousin, J. B. Jenkinson, as Bishop of St David's in 1825, but otherwise concurs with this self-assessment, writing that Liverpool was even more insistent than Pitt 'on high standards of scholarship, impeccable moral respectability and a conscientious performance of pastoral duties'. However, Liverpool had reckoned without the determinedly churlish pen of Disraeli, who claimed in his favourite novel *Tancrod*, published in 1847, that Liverpool 'sought for the successors of the apostles, for the stewards of the mysteries of Sinai and Calvary, among third-rate hunters after syllables' and thus appointed 'mitred nullities'.

It was in another of his novels, *Coningsby*, published in 1844, that Disraeli most famously and unflatteringly described Lord Liverpool as 'the Arch-Mediocrity who presided rather than ruled over' a 'Cabinet of Mediocrities'. 'In the conduct of public affairs,' Disraeli continued, 'his disposition was exactly the reverse of that which is the characteristic of great men. He was peremptory in little matters, and great ones he left open.'

Temperamentally, Liverpool was certainly not to Disraeli's liking. There was nothing of the flamboyant showman in his personality, and his speeches and conversation represent relatively poor fare when compared with Disraeli's own gift for a striking phrase, of which 'the Arch-Mediocrity' is but one example. It is also worth bearing in mind, when attempting to assess what weight to attach to Disraeli's assessment of Liverpool, that he might be expected to have been ill-disposed to the man who had nurtured the talents of the man whom Disraeli regarded as having singularly failed to appreciate his own: namely, Robert Peel.

Disraeli's critique of Liverpool should not, however, be dismissed out of hand. Certainly in so far as Liverpool turned his back, to the best of his ability, on the questions of Catholic emancipation and parliamentary reform, the charge that he left great matters open would appear to be incontestable. However, if this was not statesmanlike it was certainly politic, as can be seen from the unholy mess which the Tory party got into when Liverpool left the political stage and both of these subjects came to occupy its centre between 1827 and 1832.

Again, a case can be made for the proposition that Liverpool was an 'Arch-Mediocrity', particularly if it is argued that the supposedly repressive policies associated with the earlier years of his administration achieved nothing or even exacerbated the situation. On the other hand, Liverpool's reputation may be defended by arguing that the constructive measures passed under his leadership offset the repressive policies, which in turn may be defended as justified by the perceived threat of revolution and as effective in meeting that threat. It might even be argued, as above, that to characterise measures such as the partial suspension of Habeas Corpus in 1817–8 and the Six Acts of 1819 as repressive is misleading.

However, it is the case against Liverpool which will be reviewed prior to an examination of what may be said in his defence.

Spencer Perceval might have gone on to enjoy a long and successful tenure of office had an assassin's bullet not removed him from the scene and thereby given Liverpool his chance to form a ministry. Liverpool was arguably also the recipient of good fortune in so far as Napoleon's ill-fated invasion of Russia occurred a bare sixteen days after Liverpool became Prime Minister. The Iberian peninsula – the centre of British operations on land – was essentially a sideshow.

Liverpool's ministry was thus initially associated with a turn in the tide and successful conclusion of a long and hard-fought war. Moreover, as the nation which had most consistently and successfully opposed France, Britain enjoyed exceptionally high prestige in the councils of Europe, and she was able to capitalise upon this fact by acquiring numerous colonies at the peace treaties of 1814–15 (including the Cape of Good Hope, Ceylon, Mauritius, Trinidad, Tobago, St Lucia and Malta), which strengthened her position as the premier naval and imperial power in the world.

Liverpool arguably failed, however, to grasp what the social and economic developments of preceding decades really meant; he thus failed to exploit fully the advantages arising from Britain's colonial and naval dominance.

Moreover, a lack of imagination was compounded by clumsiness in the execution of policies, such as demobilising servicemen with such haste that they merely added to the already glutted market for labour, and over-reacting to popular unrest. Indeed, Liverpool's government can be accused of either causing or aggravating this discontent, most notably by the 1815 Corn Law, which artifically raised the price of the staple element in the diet of the common people.

And if Liverpool cannot be blamed for the 1816 repeal of the income tax, in as much as his planned retention was outvoted by his own backbenchers, the government can certainly be accused of mishandling its case in at least three respects.

First, by announcing on 9 February 1815 that discontinuation of the tax was dependent upon ratification of the Treaty of Ghent by the American Senate, the government appeared to vindicate the popular view that it was only a wartime levy. In the event, it was Napoleon's escape from Elba that persuaded the Commons to approve retention of the income tax for a further year.

Second, the substantial concessions which the Exchequer proposed, and which included lowering the standard rate from two shillings to one shilling in the pound so as to relinquish £7,500,00 of revenue per annum, were announced far too late to have any chance of countering the arguments of those favouring repeal.

Third, the government failed to make the most of those arguments in favour of the tax which MPs might have found persuasive, such as the claim that it offered the prospect of deriving a steady and growing revenue from trade at a time when this appeared better able to make a contribution to the national coffers than the landed interest.

As if the failure to retain the income tax was not bad enough in upsetting the government's fiscal policy, it made matters worse by its needless abandonment of the war tax on malt (alone worth £2,500,000 per annum). This led ultimately to the levying in 1819 of £3,000,000 in indirect taxes, including higher taxes on tobacco, coffeee, tea, cocoa and pepper, which bore down disproportionately hard on the poor. So harsh was the plight of the working class and so seemingly indifferent to that plight was Liverpool's administration, in adding to their burdens and responding to protest with repression, that the peaceful nature of much popular protest in this period can be regarded as remarkable.

And whilst it is true that the Cato Street conspiracy might seem to provide retrospective justification for the Six Acts, the role of *agents provocateurs* in inciting unrest and the small number of Spencean extremists shows that there was actually no real justification for the restrictions placed upon freedom of assembly and freedom of the press.

Moreover, even if there was more reform after 1822 and even if that reform can be attributed to the government, it can be argued that the major reforms which occurred after 1827 strongly suggest that Liverpool acted as an obstacle to, rather than as a conduit for, reform.

Having examined the case for the prosecution, the defence of Liverpool's record as premier might begin by pointing out that when Liverpool entered office as Prime Minister, Britain was still engaged in the longest war in living memory, which not only made unprecedented demands on the British state and its citizens, but was also being fought against a backdrop of domestic pressures, arising from the agricultural and industrial revolutions, which were completely without precedent.

As Secretary for War and the Colonies and as Prime Minister, Liverpool gave full material and moral support for Wellington, and whilst it is true that the British war effort in the Iberian peninsula could not inflict a mortal blow against Napoleon, the 'Spanish ulcer' did provide the most effective means of exerting pressure on France, sapping her strength and encouraging Britain's continental allies.

The abortive attempt to retain the income tax in 1816 shows that Liverpool was capable of taking statesmanlike action but that he was fatally hampered by a lack of both patronage and party discipline to ensure a stable majority in support of government policy. Indeed, the Commons was arguably less easily managed by the executive at this period than had ever been the case or was ever to be the case again.

Liverpool's critics could certainly claim that he must bear some of the responsibility for the lack of patronage at his government's disposal, as he personally played a leading role in its reduction. However, this is to ignore the fact that the Younger Pitt had given the cause of 'economical reform' such momentum that the only option available to those in office was either to jump on the bandwagon or be mown down by the juggernaut of retrenchment.

The policy of so-called 'repression' was more than simply a device of Liverpool's to curry favour with jittery backbenchers. The first duty of any government is the maintenance of law and order and governments in the early nineteenth century acknowledged few additional duties. There was thus very good reason for Liverpool, aware of popular hardship and the intellectual ferment created by the French Revolution, and lacking a sizeable standing army or police force – and accordingly dependent upon the information of spies and informers – to fear unrest. Whatever the precise role of *agents provocateurs*, incidents such as the 1816 Spa Fields riot, 1817 Pentrich rising and 1820 Cato Street conspiracy show that the government's fears of insurrection were not completely unfounded, however small the numbers involved and however unrealistic or even farcical their plots may appear in retrospect. Although Peterloo is of miniscule importance in the overall context of evaluating Liverpool's prime ministership, it has assumed a disproportionate importance in the literature of the period and is worth examining for that reason.

Whilst Peterloo cannot be condoned, it is worth stressing that the 'massacre' resulted from the misjudgment of the men on the spot, who acted in a manner directly contrary to Home Office advice. Furthermore, whilst it may have been ignoble for the government to have backed the Manchester magistrates after the event, to have chosen the course of easy popularity with the masses and condemned their actions, as the Whigs did, would have risked even greater bloodshed by undermining the authority of those in the localities upon whom the daily maintenance of law and order – and much else – largely devolved.

At a time when the penal code (largely as a consequence of the weakness of the agencies of law enforcement) was draconian, the basic moderation of the government's response to unrest is easily overlooked. As John Derry has remarked in relation to the Six Acts, 'what is surprising is not their savagery but their restraint in the light of the situation'.

Having weathered a series of squalls, the Liverpool government entered into a more constructive phase after 1821. Liverpool deserves credit for this in so far as he had pointed the way earlier, notably by his speech in favour of free trade in 1820, and by virtue of the fact that he overcame resistance to Canning's appointment from both the court and the cabinet and generally provided conditions which enabled his ministers to attend fruitfully to their departmental business.

So far from presiding over a 'Cabinet of Mediocrities', Liverpool assembled a team of enormous talent, as suggested by the fact that it contained no fewer than four future Prime Ministers: Canning, Robinson, Wellington and Peel. Moreover, the fact that such highly talented but incompatible personalities managed to work together at all was due to Liverpool's diplomacy. Rather than 'the Arch-Mediocrity' he was the arch-mediator.

No politician can survive without luck but Liverpool was not always blessed by good fortune. If he had the good fortune that Napoleon invaded Russia a mere sixteen days after he entered office, he had already had the misfortune that the United States had declared war on Great Britain five days before this.

However, luck alone cannot account for Liverpool's political longevity. To get to the top of the 'greasy pole' – even for someone with Liverpool's advantages of birth – is, as Disraeli might more charitably have acknowledged, no mean achievement in itself, and to occupy that position for fifteen years and only leave it as a result of ill-health strengthens the *a priori* case against Disraeli's characterisation of Liverpool as 'the Arch-Mediocrity'. The reasons for Liverpool's staying power will now be subjected to scrutiny.

Liverpool's political lifetime, and the years of his premiership in particular, were marked by the emergence of an articulate and critical, broadly middle-class, public opinion, which, notwithstanding any defects of the unreformed parliament, was increasingly recognised and reflected, albeit in refracted form, in the House of Commons. This posed relatively few problems for Liverpool's premiership because, as has already been mentioned, the war with France resulted in Liverpool's regime's being bathed in the flattering light of military victories, colonial acquisitions and high international prestige in its early years. The war, moreover, distracted attention away from more divisive domestic issues and divided the parliamentary opposition to Liverpool, as the Grenvillites urged the vigorous prosecution of the war whilst the Foxite Whigs still hankered after peace with Napoleonic France.

The Grenvillite–Foxite alliance was further weakened by the fact that Grenville's successor as head of this pro-Catholic political connection or clan, his nephew, the Duke of Buckingham, was not so close to Grey, and – like the overwhelming majority of independent MPs – was sympathetic towards Liverpool's firm line in response to public disorder. He was, moreover, ambitious for office.

Hence the Grenvillites detached themselves from the Foxite Whigs in 1818, to sit as a separate group, and formally agreed to join Liverpool's ministry in December 1821. The adhesion of the Grenvillites not only reunited the Pittite coalition of 1801 but also deprived the king of any choice of alternative ministry other than an exclusively Whig one.

This rallying of Grenvillite support to the government in the face of popular unrest was also part of a broader process that witnessed a strengthening of support for the government amongst the independent members in the Commons and amongst the propertied within the country at large. Even more general contentment with Liverpool's administration resulted from the general return to prosperity after 1822.

Furthermore, Grey's inactivity (staying at home in 1814 and 1816, announcing his intention to withdraw from active politics in 1817, and gradual withdrawal culminating in his informal resignation as leader in 1826) and the undistinguished nature of the Whig leaders in the Commons, George Ponsonby (until 1817) and George Tierney (from 1818 until 1821), weakened the Whigs still further. According to Mitchell, the Whigs' leadership problem was only successfully resolved in 1830.

Liverpool, by contrast, provided strong but subtle leadership, possessing political arts and not just luck, which made him indispensable to the Tories. As someone who could not be neatly categorised as either a High or Low Tory but who was sympathetic towards elements of both viewpoints and respected by both sections of the party, he was ideally placed to hold the party together. Both wings saw him as an acceptable leader who had something to offer in policy terms, with opposition to Catholic emancipation counterbalanced by his willingness to countenance commercial and legal reforms, for example. Brock does not exaggerate when he writes that Liverpool 'was certainly the only man who could hold together the Cabinet between 1822 and 1827'.

His withdrawal from politics as a result of a stroke on 17 February 1827 soon showed him, in Boyd Hilton's words, to have been 'the indispensable operator of the political machine'. This machine, moreover was much more difficult to operate than that of earlier or later years. He lacked the powers of patronage enjoyed by his eighteenth-century counterparts and the effective control of his party which nineteenth-century party leaders were able to wield. He had also to cope with monarchs who were held in general disrespect and with a dearth of debating talent on the government front bench in the Commons. All this meant that he faced much greater problems than his predecessors or successors had to confront.

As Gash puts it, Liverpool's government was not only 'the last of the great eighteenth-century administrations in its structure and duration' but also 'the first of the great nineteenth-century administrations in its problems and achievements'.

There were certainly also other constraints upon Liverpool's room for manoeuvre. The war until 1815, the transition to peace with the accompanying problems of deflation and domestic unrest until 1819, and then the Queen Caroline affair in the years 1820–21 tended to monopolise the government's attention and energies, whilst Canning, and to a lesser extent Huskisson, represented a continual drain upon Liverpool's personal reserves of energy and goodwill in so far as their restlessness and lack of tact obliged him to be constantly defending their actions to their distrustful colleagues.

Despite all this Liverpool was also very successful in his attempt to keep contentious policy decisions – most notably the question of Catholic emancipation – out of the political arena.

After all, Liverpool's government was based upon the so-called 'open' system, whereby ministers could express their individual views on the matter of Catholic emancipation but the government as such remained studiously neutral on the issue.

This situation worked very well until 1821, when Plunket's proposed measure of relief for Catholics revealed there to be a small pro-Catholic majority in the Commons and a large anti-Catholic majority in the Lords. It is in this context that Liverpool's admission of the Grenvillites to the ministry should be appreciated, for he thereby not only effectively neutralised them as pro-Catholics (since their acceptance of office obliged them to adopt the 'open' system) but also used them to balance the anti-Catholic appointments in the reconstructed ministry, as Goulburn became Irish Chief Secretary, Peel became Home Secretary, and Sidmouth retained a place at the cabinet table as Minister without Portfolio.

Canning's Catholic Peers' Bill of April 1822 to allow Catholics to sit in the House of Lords can thus be viewed as an attempt by the former President of the Board of Control to persuade his former cabinet colleagues that it would be advisable for them to invite him to return to office – a prospect which was rendered even more desirable following the suicide of the pro-Catholic Castlereagh in August 1822.

Although Boyd Hilton has convincingly argued that the elevations of Canning and Huskisson to the cabinet in 1822–3 rendered the strategy of avoiding contentious policy issues difficult, if not impossible, to maintain in the long term, Liverpool certainly succeeded in the short term in defusing the emancipation issue, as shown by the fact that in 1823 Plunket was forced to abandon another motion for Catholic relief for lack of support in the Commons. However, the emergence of O'Connell's Catholic Association galvanised the emancipation lobby so that when Burdett introduced a motion on 28 February 1825 for a committee of the whole House to consider Catholic claims, the motion was passed by thirteen votes and Liverpool and Peel (the only anti-Catholic cabinet member in the Commons) began to speak privately of resignation. This course of action was no longer considered necessary, and the 'open' system was restored with a renewed mandate, when the Lords threw out Burdett's bill by forty-eight votes.

Last but not least, in assessing Liverpool's staying power it

should be noted that he never lost the confidence of the sovereign, although it would be more accurate to say that George IV's
confidence in Liverpool never plummeted so far as to overcome
his natural indolence and political timidity. Thus threats of
dismissal remained nothing more than threats.

Several historians, including Derry, Evans, Gash and Parry,
argue that the growth of collective cabinet solidarity and responsibility under Liverpool's premiership was decisive in en-
abling him to manage the King, as this development rendered it
almost certain that dismissal of Liverpool would result in the
resignation of his cabinet colleagues.

There is certainly evidence to support the view that Liverpool's premiership was marked by the growth of the principle
of collective responsibility and its corollary of collective resignation. Thus Liverpool himself informed Arbuthnot in October
1823 that 'The K[ing] will find himself very much mistaken if
he supposes that if he dismissed me . . . Canning, Peel, or anyone
of my colleagues would remain behind'.

However, against this must first be set the peculiar position of
the Duke of Wellington, whose authority as the victor of Waterloo gave him a position above day-to-day politics and enabled
him to express the view repeatedly that he would not feel bound,
in certain circumstances, to follow Liverpool out of office.

Moreover, in the aftermath of the Queen Caroline affair
Liverpool himself had not been sanguine regarding the support
of his cabinet colleagues, confiding to Arbuthnot that 'I will not
abandon others but I am by no means sure that they will not
abandon me and leave me to be the *sole* victim of the present
clamour'.

Boyd Hilton's illuminating article on the political arts of Lord
Liverpool reminds us that in pursuit of his policy of keeping
contentious policy issues out of the political arena whenever
possible, Liverpool in any case largely by-passed the cabinet in
policy making, stuffing it with 'ornamental' members such as
Mulgrave, Westmorland and Bragge-Bathurst, hardly ever calling it to meet during the recess, sending out invitations hap-
hazardly, not always bothering to attend himself, and providing
no agendas or briefings, no minutes and often no record of
decisions taken. Matters improved somewhat after 1823 but to
speak of the cabinet as a cohesive and businesslike body in this
period is to overstate the case.

The absence of any settled convention of collective cabinet action makes Liverpool's achievements even more remarkable. When one also takes into account the fact that after fifteen years Liverpool's administration was, to quote Gash, 'more popular in the country, more firmly entrenched in the good opinion of Parliament and the Crown, than at any previous time' and that when Liverpool left office he was poorer than when he entered it, yet left Britain more prosperous, more stable and more respected as a power, then one has some measure of the greatness of his achievement.

7

Conclusion: the legacy of Liverpool's premiership

In his highly stimulating book *The Rise and Fall of Liberal Government in Victorian Britain*, Jonathan Parry argues that after 1815 two processes laid the foundations for the Liberal governments which dominated early and mid-Victorian Britain, namely, the rise of the notion of a virtuous, middle-class 'public opinion' and an increasing ministerial awareness of the desirability of creating a more open, streamlined and economical state.

Parry credits Canning with a key role in responding to, and satisfying, these demands, arguing that the Tories in the 1820s made 'significant changes in the substance and presentation of politics'. More specifically, Parry claims that Canning presented 'liberal' government as involving 'the claim to be responsive to virtuous public and parliamentary sentiment' with a resultant 'emphasis on economy, commercial expansion and administrative reform; the distancing of ministers from royal power and corrupt patronage networks' and 'the encouragement of constitutional principles abroad'.

Opinions differ over the extent to which the changes referred to above were substantive rather than purely presentational but Parry is certainly right to emphasise the limits to Canning's liberalism when he argues that Canning's conception of liberal government was presented in such a way as to pre-empt the demand for parliamentary reform, on the grounds that the unreformed parliament was already perfectly responsive to public demands for openness, economy and morality. However, 'by raising public expectations of government so high, he placed his successors in a difficulty, which was to prove particularly acute when economic conditions were not so rosy and dissatisfaction therefore not so easily assuaged'.

What the above does not make due allowance for, however, is the fact that the brand of Toryism associated with Liverpool, which some have labelled 'Liberal Toryism', did not even survive Liverpool's stroke, as shown by the dissolution of the coalition achieved and maintained by Liverpool when Canning became prime minister and the failure of Canning's attempt to modify the Corn Laws in March 1827, despite the fact that Liverpool's cabinet had approved the scheme as recently as November 1826.

The broad church Toryism of Lord Liverpool was doomed not by any deterioration in the economy but by virtue of the fact that Canning's liberal Toryism was too liberal for many Tories to swallow in so far as he was identified with a demand for radical constitutional reform, in the shape of Catholic emancipation, which, as the events of 1827–32 were to show, was regarded by many Tories as even more objectionable than parliamentary reform.

In the period between Liverpool's stroke and the invitation from the king for Canning to form a government, Burdett's general resolution on the Catholic question was defeated by four votes: the first pro-Catholic motion to fail to pass the Commons since 1819. This fact no doubt made it easier for Canning to accept the king's desire that the government should continue on its 'open' basis when Canning replaced Liverpool. However, the refusal of half of Liverpool's cabinet, including Wellington and Peel, to serve under Canning forced him to recruit from the Whigs. Moreover, the balance which Liverpool had so painstakingly maintained had shifted even further in the pro-Catholic direction with nine pro-Catholics and just three anti-Catholics in Canning's cabinet compared with eight and six respectively in his predecessor's, and Canning found himself unable to meet the King's wishes for either an anti-Catholic Home Secretary or an anti-Catholic Irish Chief Secretary.

Thus Canning proved incapable of holding together the Tory party fashioned by Liverpool. Parry nevertheless claims that 'the "liberal toryism" of the 1820s was to be a major influence on Liberal history' as 'many of Canning's followers were to switch sides and become important Liberals'. Continuing liberal Tory influence is also claimed by Gash, as he regards the fiscal and commercial policies of 1841–6 as 'identical' in philosophy and objective with those pursued under Liverpool in the 1820s, the Whig decade of the 1830s being 'a mere interlude in the continuity of economic policy between Liverpool and Peel'.

If accurate, this latter assessment might at least help to explain the intensity of Disraeli's dislike of Liverpool. Gash argues that despite Disraeli's jaundiced assessment, liberal Tory influence did in fact extend to the Disraelian Conservative party and beyond, for whilst 'the myth of conservatism has been more often Disraelian, its practice has been almost uniformly Peelite'.

This contest to claim descent from the Tory party in the 1820s shows three things: that the liberal, free-trade Victorian state had its roots in the 1820s; that the differences between the Gladstonian Liberal and Disraelian Conservative parties were not so great as appears at first sight; and that historians, no less than politicians, often succumb to the temptation of 'body-snatching'.

Select bibliography

M. Bentley, *Politics Without Democracy, 1815–1914* (London: Fontana, 1984), N. Gash, *Aristocracy and People, 1815–65* (London: Arnold, 1979) and J. Parry, *The Rise and Fall of Liberal Government in Victorian Britain* (London: Yale University Press, 1993) have a high 'political–culture entry fee' compared with: D. E. D. Beales, *From Castlereagh to Gladstone 1815–1885* (Walton-on-Thames: Thomas Nelson, 1969), R. Brown, *Church and State in Modern Britain 1700–1850* (London: Routledge, 1991) and Eric J. Evans, *The Forging of the Modern State* (London: Longman, 1983) but these all provide useful introductions to the period.

T. S. Ashton, *The Industrial Revolution 1760–1830* (Oxford: Oxford University Press, 1968), R. Brown, *Society and Economy in Modern Britain 1700–1850* (London: Routledge, 1991) and W. Rostow, *The Stages of Economic Growth* (Cambridge: Cambridge University Press, 1960) shed light on the economic background whilst the period's social unrest is best covered by J. Stevenson, *Popular Disturbances in England 1700–1832* (London: Longman, 1992, 2nd edn).

E. J. Hobsbawm's *The Crowd in History* (New York: John Wiley, 1964) and E. P. Thompson's *The Making of the English Working Class* (London: Pelican, 1968) have been very influential and have superseded the work of earlier social historians such as J. L. Hammond and B. Hammond (authors of the trilogy

The Village Labourer, The Town Labourer and *The Skilled Labourer*: London: Longman, 1978, 1978 and 1979 respectively) but they are just as partisan in their judgments, as is shown by J. R. Dinwiddy, *From Luddism to the First Reform Bill* (Oxford: Blackwell, 1986) and J. R. Dinwiddy, *Radicalism and Reform in Britain 1780–1850* (London: Hambledon, 1992).

R. J. White, *Waterloo to Peterloo* (London: Heinemann, 1957) which focuses on the ill-fated Derbyshire Rising of 1817 remains one of the most readable portraits of the period and its discontents. By contrast, an abstract but suggestive treatment of social unrest is to be found in J. C. Davies, 'Towards a theory of revolution' in P. G. Lewis, D. C. Potter and F. G. Castles (eds), *The Practice of Comparative Politics* (London: Longman, 1978).

J. E. Cookson, *Lord Liverpool's Administration, 1815–1822* (Edinburgh: Scottish Academic Press, 1983) has rarity value in dealing sympathetically with the supposedly reactionary years of Liverpool's government, whilst J. W. Derry, *Politics in the Age of Fox, Pitt and Liverpool* (London: Macmillan, 1990) and 'Lord Liverpool: the unobtrusive Prime Mininster', *History Sixth* Issue 20, pp. 21–6 is chiefly concerned to place Liverpool's entire adminstration in a late Hanoverian context.

D. E. D. Beales 'Peel, Russell and Reform', *The Historical Journal* Vol. 17/4 1974, pp. 873–82, presents a judicious review of some of Peel's reforms as Home Secretary, which is carried further in V. A. C. Gatrell, *The Hanging. Execution and the English People 1770–1868* (Oxford: Oxford University Press, 1994) and provides a useful corrective to N. Gash, *Mr Secretary Peel* (London: Longman, 1961).

A. Brady, *William Huskisson and Liberal Reform* (London: Frank Cass, 1967, 2nd edn) is still useful on the commercial policies of Liverpool's government despite a skewed emphasis upon imperial preference arising from its Canadian provenance. B. Gordon, *Political Economy in Parliament 1819–1823* (London: Macmillan, 1976), B. Gordon, *Economic Doctrine and Tory Liberalism 1824–1830* (London: Macmillan, 1979) and T. L. Crosby, *English Farmers and the Politics of Protection 1815–1852* (Hassocks: Harvester, 1977) should all be consulted in order to appreciate the originality of A. J. B. Hilton's *Corn, Cash, Commerce. The Economic Policies of the Tory Governments 1815–1830* (Oxford: Oxford University Press, 1977), which anticipates his *Age of Atonement* (Oxford: Oxford University Press, 1988) in its pioneering analysis of the relationship between economic and religious thought.

A. J. B. Hilton's 'The political arts of Lord Liverpool', *Transactions of the Royal Historical Society* (1988, pp. 147–70) is also the best account of Liverpool's political skills.

The most divisive issue of the day is comprehensively analysed in G. I. T. Machin, *The Catholic Question in English Politics 1820 to 1830* (Oxford: Oxford University Press, 1964), and J. Cannon (ed.), *The Whig Ascendancy* (London: Edward Arnold, 1981) is of value in setting in context A. Mitchell, *The Whigs in Opposition 1815–1830* (Oxford: Oxford University Press, 1967) and E. A. Smith, *Whig Principles and Party Politics. Earl Fitzwilliam and the Whig Party 1748–1833* (Manchester: Manchester University Press, 1975).

N. Gash, *Lord Liverpool. The Life and Political Career of Robert Banks Jenkinson 2nd Earl of Liverpool 1770–1828* (London: Weidenfeld, 1984) is the only modern biography of Liverpool. It is stronger on the times than the man and Gash himself admits that a larger-scale biography based upon the archival materials still needs to be written. Useful articles on Liverpool in addition to those already mentioned include Eric J. Evans, 'The Premiership of Lord Liverpool' *History Sixth* April 1990 pp. 13–14, and N. Gash, 'Lord Liverpool' in H. Van Thal (ed.), *The Prime Ministers. Sir Robert Walpole to Sir Robert Peel* (London: Allen and Unwin, 1974), 'Lord Liverpool: A Private View' *History Today* May 1990, pp. 35–40) and 'The Tortoise and the Hare: Liverpool and Canning' *History Today* March 1992, pp. 12–19.

Primary sources on the period can be found in Eric J. Evans, *Britain Before the Reform Act: Politics and Society 1815–1832* (London: Longman, 1989), P. Revill, *The Age of Lord Liverpool* (Glasgow: Blackie, 1979) and E. A. Smith, *A Queen on Trial. The Affair of Queen Caroline* (Dover: Alan Sutton, 1993). The first of these (a volume in the *Seminar Studies* series) is not only the broadest in scope but the best, in so far as it does not allow the documents to obscure the author's interpretation.

Last but not least, W. R. Brock, *Lord Liverpool and Liberal Toryism* (Cambridge, Cambridge University Press, 1941) still deserves to be read not only as the classic exposition of the now-discredited doctrine of Liberal Toryism and the argument that the cabinet changes of 1821–3 constituted a watershed in the nature of Liverpool's government, but also because of the light which it sheds on Liverpool's personality and the character of his administration.